GLOBE QUARTOS

THE POOR MAN'S COMFORT

ROBERT DABORNE

First printed: London, 1655

This edition prepared by Jane Kingsley-Smith

GLOBE EDUCATION

NHB

NICK HERN BOOKS
LONDON

www.nickhernbooks.co.uk

GLOBE QUARTOS

This edition of *The Poor Man's Comfort*
first published in Great Britain
as a paperback original in 2005
by Nick Hern Books Limited
14 Larden Road, London W3 7ST

in association with

Globe Education
Shakespeare's Globe, New Globe Walk
London, SE1 9DT

Copyright in this edition © 2005
International Shakespeare Globe Centre Ltd

Printed by CLE Print Ltd, St Ives, Cambridgeshire PE27 3LE

A CIP catalogue record for this book is available from
the British Library

ISBN 1 85459 802 3

Preface

In 1744/5, Robert Dodsley sought to "snatch some of the best pieces of our old Dramatic Writers from total Neglect and Oblivion". He published sixty-one plays, written before the death of Charles I, in a *Select Collection of Old Plays* in twelve volumes.

In 1995, Globe Education decided to follow Dodsley's example and initiated a 30-year project to stage readings and record, with professional casts, all the non-Shakespeare plays written for the stage between 1567 and 1642. To date, audiences have been able to hear over 120 plays by Barnes, Haughton, Shirley, Wilkins et al.

Full productions of Beaumont and Fletcher's *The Maid's Tragedy* and Middleton's *A Chaste Maid in Cheapside* were staged in the Globe Theatre's opening season in 1997. Since then, Mark Rylance, the Globe's artistic director, has included a second Middleton play as well as plays by Marlowe and Brome in Globe Theatre Seasons.

The popularity of both readings and productions prompted Globe Education to approach Nick Hern to publish some of the plays that had been revived. The first *Globe Quarto* was edited by Nick de Somogyi and published in 1998. An Editorial Board, composed of David Scott Kastan, Gordon McMullan and Richard Proudfoot, was established to oversee the series in 1999. Thomas L. Berger and Martin White are now joint general-editors.

Globe Education is indebted to all the *Globe Quarto* editors and to everyone who has helped give new life to old plays in staged readings and in productions. The plays and the editions only have a life, however, if they have an audience and readers. I am therefore grateful to you for buying this edition.

As Dodsley noted to his patron, "but for your Generosity" these plays would have "faln with their Authors into utter Oblivion".

Patrick Spottiswoode
Director, Globe Education

Editorial Board's Preface

The plays are presented in texts based on the most reliable originals (usually the first printed editions) fully modernised so as to make them easily usable by modern actors and readers. Editorial correction and emendation is undertaken as required by the state of the original. Extra stage directions, and additions to those of the original that are needed to make the action clear, are enclosed in square brackets. In verse speeches, apostrophes to indicate elision of vowels and accents to indicate where a word should be stressed are used where appropriate as a guide to metre. In particular, the ending '-ed' in participles and past tenses of verbs is retained only where it is to be pronounced as a separate syllable (or after 'i' or ''u', as in 'tried', and 'sued'); otherwise it appears as '-'d'.

Introductory matter includes notes from the director or co-ordinator of the production or reading of the play at the Globe and a brief factual introduction by the editor. Glossarial Notes (more comprehensive than in earlier Globe Quartos and keyed to the text by line numbers) explain difficult or obsolete usages and offer brief comment on other points of interest or obscurity. Departures from the wording of the original are recorded in Textual Notes that identify the source of corrections or editorial emendations. The opening page of the text in the original on which the edition is based is reproduced in facsimile. Extra material relevant to understanding the play may occasionally be included in an Appendix.

Acknowledgements

My main debt of thanks is to my general editor, Gordon McMullan, for all his valuable counsel, patiently given. I would also like to thank Tom Berger for the penetrating eye he cast over the edition in its final stages. I am grateful too for suggestions made by Martin Wiggins and Peter Hinds.

The work of earlier editors of *The Poor Man's Comfort*, particularly Kenneth Palmer's Malone Society reprint, has made a significant contribution to this edition and is gratefully acknowledged here. Finally, I would like to thank the British Library for permission to reprint the first text page of one of the 1655 quartos.

Jane Kingsley-Smith
Editor

A Note from the Co-ordinator of the Staged Reading

As an actor, I have been involved in several of the rehearsed readings undertaken by the Globe Education department and have been greatly inspired by these lesser-known gems from the Renaissance treasure trove.

When offered the opportunity to co-ordinate one myself, I was thrilled and accepted the challenge. "What is The Poor Man's Comfort, then?", was a question I was frequently asked by friends and family as I began my research. "Justice", I replied.

Daborne's play – the source of which can be traced back to William Warner's *Pan his Syrinx* (1584) – is a didactic one and often seems to emulate the style of the sermon. (It is no surprise that Daborne later took vows, joining the ranks of Donne and Herbert as 17th century poet-priests). Sifting through the story, I discovered many biblical – as well as mythological – references which influenced my approach in terms of visual vocabulary, tone and casting. Intensive research was necessary for such a staged reading because cast and crew (Vastine Stabler) had only five hours to accomplish what would usually take four to six weeks.

On the day? I felt exhilarated and perhaps a little intimidated. After all, many of the actors were far more experienced. I am deeply thankful to them for their generosity and patience. With a props list that included straw hats, empty toaster boxes, confetti, flowers for lapels, passports for epistles, a bottle of aspirin, bags of autumn leaves, rubber fish and assorted amphibia, we had to recreate such scenes as a country wedding (plus choreographed barn dance), a shipwreck, the business of the senate and our own 'Pythonesque' homage to the mysteries of Masonic ritual.

Nick Tigg and I worked closely on the incidental music. Instruments included mandolin, ukulele and guitar, as well as the all-humbling and pomp-popping kazoo to herald in the King. The ensemble created off-stage as well as on-stage vocal effects: the bleating sheep, bird-song, crickets, frogs, a barking dog, gerbils (don't ask!), a gale, the sea, bats and whispering.

Many of the characters posed new challenges for the actors. Urania's libidinous restraint may not be a quality that is immediately recognisable to the contemporary female! However, in the context of our play, and bearing in mind that the Women's Property Act was yet to be fought for, it serves as a sharp contrast to Flavia's duplicitous 'gold-digging' which ultimately signals her undoing. This dichotomy is only balanced by the arrival of Adelizia, who is predestined to marry Sigismond only after a spell as anchoress in the untamed dominion of the forest. This trio of female stereotypes can only be appreciated if they are embraced as one complete being and thus the play is saved from the fate of reductive thinking often associated with literature of this period.

Sigismond's allusion to *Richard III* in the lines 'my kingdom for a boat' points to the lightness of touch with which Daborne tackles his weighty socio-political concerns. Gisbert's reenactment of the rhetorical platitudes as spouted by the senators in Act 3 scene 1 is one of the most fascinating scenes on the page and (as played by Derek Smith) was a tour de force on the stage, giving the audience an opportunity to witness the character's innate ingenuity and eloquence through the vehicle of satire.

Daborne gave his Assize sermon at Waterford between 1617 and 1618. It is intriguing to imagine how *The Poor Man's Comfort* may have paved the way for it.

There is much for the reader to enjoy in the language as characters try to judge between one thing and another: to part right from wrong, truth from falsehood. All in all, as was observable in the fine performances throughout and made explicit in the final denouement, the life of the play is in its core conviction that justice ought not to be a mere weighing of the facts on the scales of the intellectual, but rests firmly on our ability to interpret the divine will.

Liza Hayden

The Poor Man's Comfort

Cast of the play, adapted and co-ordinated by Liza Hayden, which was performed at Shakespeare's Globe on 24 March 2002.

Ferdinand, King of Thessaly	Christopher Godwin
Sigismond, his son	James Albrecht
Oswell, the rebel	Callum Coates
Vincentio, a senator	Bill Bingham
Silleus, a senator	Robert Wilby
Leonardo, a senator	Stephen Jenn
Glisco, a senator	Robert Whitelock
Lucius, a noble man of Thessaly	Jules Werner
Jaspero, a courtier	Jason Baron
Licurgo, a courtier	Robert Whitelock
Gisbert, the poor man, a shepherd	Derek Smith
Cosmo, a rich shepherd	Robert Wilby
Surdo, his son, the clown	Garry Roost
Lysippus, an honest shepherd	Stephen Jenn
Alexis, his son	Matt Jamie
Catzo, the fool	Nick Wilton
Adelizia, daughter to the King of Sicily	Dominique Biscomb
Urania, the fair shepherdess	Frog Stone
Mrs. Gullman, a bawd	Ishia Bennison
Flavia, her daughter, a whore	Sarah Corbett
Musician	Nicholas Tigg

Editor's Introduction

The earliest reference to Robert Daborne's involvement with the Jacobean stage occurs in 1610; a licence issued for the Children of the Queen's Revels authorises Daborne and his colleagues to 'bring up and practice children in plays' (*DNB*). However, by this date Daborne may already have begun his career as a playwright, working alone and in collaboration on at least seven plays, though only two – *A Christian Turned Turk* and *The Poor Man's Comfort* – have survived.

Daborne was probably born *c.* 1580-3 and matriculated at King's College, Cambridge in 1598 where he may also have been awarded an MA. The title-page of *A Christian Turned Turk* describes the author as a 'gentleman' and he was probably related to the Dabornes who owned land and property in Surrey. Nevertheless, the playwright's father died in debt and Daborne was to be dogged by financial hardship and law-suits throughout his theatrical career. In 1609, he moved, with his pregnant wife, Anne, and children, into a house in Shoreditch belonging to Anne's father, Robert Younger. A subsequent Chancery suit recalls that 'the distresse of the said Dawborne at that tyme was soe exceedinge great that he had noe settled dwellinge place, and that his povertie was such that for want of money and freinds [*sic*] he could not provide necessaries for him selfe his wyfe and children' (Phelps, 4).

This theme of impecunity also recurs in the letters Daborne wrote to the theatrical entrepreneur, Philip Henslowe, between April 1613 and July 1614. Here, Daborne asks Henslowe for money on the receipt of sheets of script, sent off as soon as he had written them. Works then in progress, now lost, include *Machiavel and the Devil*, a collaboration with Tourneur called *The Arraignment of London*, *The Owl* and *The She-Saint*. Daborne seems to have been aware that his method of composition – rapid, fragmentary, working simultaneously on multiple plays – did not necessarily facilitate great art. In December 1613, he wrote to Henslowe of his hope that 'howsoever my want informs me for a tyme, I shall shortly be out of it & be able to forbear a play till I can make the best' (Greg, 79). We cannot know whether Daborne ever felt that he had achieved this. Yet *The Poor Man's Comfort* seems at least to have found some popular acclaim. The title-page to the first published edition (a quarto in 1655) describes it as 'The Poor-Mans Comfort. A Tragi-Comedy, As it was divers times Acted at the Cock-pit in Drury Lane with great applause'.

The Poor Man's Comfort was probably composed between 1615 and 1617 when a reference to the Porter's Hall theatre and its threatened closure (2.3.50) would have been topical. Certainly, it was finished before February 1618 as from this date onwards Daborne was in Ireland, having been ordained as a minister. The first performances of the play, performed by the Queen Anne's Men, probably took place at the Red Bull theatre before transferring to the Cock-pit theatre in Drury Lane after 1617.

Daborne had seen one play through the presses: *A Christian Turned Turk* in 1612. In his preface 'To the Knowing Reader', he states that publication is a means of recouping lost theatrical revenues and of defending his own reputation, suggesting that the play had been banned following accusations of slander. With no such pressing motive for the publication of *The Poor Man*, and with his mind perhaps already on a higher, spiritual vocation, Daborne left the superior play unpublished. Hence, it is not until 1655 that *The Poor Man's Comfort* first appears in print.

Although twenty-seven years after Daborne's death, the date of this publication is not altogether surprising. In the late 1640s and 1650s, we see a number of Jacobean works appearing in print for the first time by playwrights including Thomas Middleton, Thomas Dekker, Francis Beaumont and John Fletcher. Yet there are other reasons why an interregnum reader might have cast a favourable eye upon this play in particular. The story of a deposed monarch, seven years in exile, who finally regains his throne – a monarch celebrated for his sympathy with the poor man of the title

– might have proven popular with royalist sympathisers, five years before the restoration of Charles II. In particular, the reference at 3.3.17 to the prince, Sigismond, as 'a good Commonwealth's man' is an irony that would only have made sense to a post-1642 audience, suggesting that the play may have been revised to make it more relevant to the 1650s reader.

Whether the 1655 quarto represents the play as originally performed or as subsequently revised, *The Poor Man's Comfort* owes debts to a variety of dramatic traditions. Gisbert's lament against injustice, his madness, and his thoughts on revenge suggest the influence of Elizabethan revenge tragedy, in particular *The Spanish Tragedy*, *Titus Andronicus* and *Hamlet*. The pastoral elements of the play, including the shipwreck of Adelizia and Lucius' disguise as a shepherd, reflect the taste for pastoral drama exemplified by Shakespeare's *As You Like It* and Daniel's *Hymen's Triumph*. There are also more peculiarly tragi-comic features including the brothel scenes, attempted murder and suicide, and the reconciliation of father and daughter. These might recall Shakespeare's late plays (in particular *Pericles*) and the work of Beaumont and Fletcher (e.g. *Philaster*). Nevertheless, the actual murder of Flavia in *The Poor Man's Comfort* and the subsequent forgiveness of her murderer, Lucius, represent the exertion of extreme pressure on the conventions of tragi-comedy. Ultimately, perhaps, it was this strange fusion of violence and bawdy, pathos and farce, which made *The Poor Man's Comfort* the most successful play of Daborne's career.

Jane Kingsley-Smith

Bibliography

A. H. Bullen, 'Daborne, Robert', *DNB* (1888)

W. W. Greg (ed.), *Henslowe Papers* (London: A. H. Bullen, 1907)

Alfred Harbage and S. Schoenbaum, *Annals of English Drama* 3rd ed. rev. by S. S. Wagonheim (London: Routledge, 1989)

Baldwin Maxwell, 'Notes on Robert Daborne's Extant Plays', *Philological Quarterly* 50 (1971), 85-98

Wayne H. Phelps, 'The Early Life of Robert Daborne', *Philological Quarterly* 59 (1980), 1-10

A. E. H. Swaen, 'Robert Daborne's Plays', *Anglia* 20 (1898), 153-256

Daniel J. Vitkus (ed.), *Three Turk Plays from Early Modern England* (includes *A Christian Turned Turk*) (New York: Columbia University Press, 2000)

The Poor Man's Comfort

Dramatis Personae

The Persons of the Play

[PROLOGUE]
FERDINAND — King of Thessaly
SIGISMOND — His son
OSWELL — The rebel
VINCENTIO — Senators
SILLEUS
LEONARDO
GLISCO
LUCIUS — A nobleman of Thessaly, fled into Arcadia (when the King was overthrown), and disguised under the name of LYSANDER, husband of URANIA

JASPERO — Courtiers
LICURGO
GISBERT — The poor man, a shepherd
COSMO — A rich shepherd
SURDO — His son, the clown
LYSIPPUS — An honest shepherd
ALEXIS — His son
CATZO — The fool, the Prince's man
ADELIZIA — Daughter to the King of Sicily
URANIA — The fair shepherdess, daughter to GISBERT, after[wards] servant to FLAVIA, disguised under the name of CASTADORA

MRS GULLMAN — A bawd
FLAVIA — Her daughter, a whore

The scene Thessaly

[*Enter*] the PROLOGUE

If, in this present, thriving age,
A poor man may become the stage,
Or if abused charity
And honest-minded poverty
May please, or if bad men ingrate
And strumpets foul adulterate,
So whipp'd and punish'd for their crimes,
At once may like and teach the times,
We have our aims. So, to your sight
The poor man offers up his might.   10

[*Exit*]

Per E. M.

1[.1]

Enter LUCIUS *like a shepherd and* URANIA *like a shepherdess*

Lucius	Stay, fair Urania, thou whose only beauty
	Would make a desert rich and force kings leave
	Their purple thrones to come and gaze at thee,
	Lysander craves thee stay – he that does dote on thee
	More than the female on her new-fall'n kid.
Urania	You should be still a flatterer by your tongue.
Lucius	By all my hopes I swear, return my love
	But that fair grace it merits and, on my faith,
	A trial, beyond which the covetous thought
	Of man ne'er went, I'll undergo 10
	And in the achievement lose myself ere thee.
Urania	You overvalue me. Were I possess'd
	Of so high passions, what you term love,
	Alexis' equal suit should sooner move
	Than you, whose birth is all unknown to me.
Lucius	Ungentle maid, let not thy cruelty
	Force me despair. He that so oft has sung
	And won the prize for dance and roundelays;
	He that has vowed his chaste thoughts to thy shrine;
	Given thee the tender firstlings of his flocks; 20
	Who, amongst the fairest lasses of the plains,
	Chose thee his prize when, at the public games,
	He crown'd thee with the wreath which, for his merit

	In songs and active sports, he did inherit	
	From the deserving swains. Do not forget	
	My seven years' service, which to attain thee yet	
	Would seem but as one summer's day.	
Urania	You are too forward.	
Lucius	True love does charge, and that fault lay on me.	
	Oh, did thy yielding heart feel but the fires!	30
Urania	[*aside*] Alas! I feel too much!	
	[*to* LUCIUS] In modesty, forbear thy violent suit	
	Which breeds suspect – true love being ever mute,	
	When lust finds means to speak.	
Lucius	Command, thou cruel maid, this heart to break	
	Which only words give life to.	
Urania	Nay, then, I fly thee, or else I shall not know –	
Lucius	How to deny me? Oh, speak that word once more.	
	[*Takes hold of her*]	
Urania	Will you enforce my love?	
Lucius	Rather than live –	
	[URANIA *tries to pull away*]	
	Stay and but hear my vow.	
	Enter GISBERT	
Gisbert	[*apart*] Whom ha' we here?	40
	Lysander and my daughter got so near?	
	Where two such chaste breasts meet, I need not fear.	

| | Some earnest suit belike; were it her love,
He merits it. She cannot but approve
His worth and person fitter for a state
Than the employment of so low a fate. |

Urania   Oh, do not wrong me so!

Lucius   I do appeal to you, who well do know
The loyal service these seven winters past
Have stood impartial witness to, if I have gain'd   50
Least happiness in aught but might express
My constant labour. Have I in excess
My master's store consum'd, or robb'd his flocks
To serve a private riot? Have I not borne the shock
Of sharpest storms to drive my weary herd
To place of shelter? Did the sun behold
The dewy plains before me, or the day's heat
Force me unto the shade? Did the robb'd females
  bleat
For loss of tender young – whilst sleep possess'd
My slothful eye – by rav'nous wolves oppress'd   60
Or time-observing fox? If, to make known
A grateful mind, I have so well begun,
Oh, think how happy, by enjoying thee,
The period of my lingering pains would be!

Gisbert   [*apart*] Thou speakest most true.
These tears that speak my love do witness it.

Urania   You well have told how much we do forget
Your labours, sir. For my part, I confess
You merit much, nor am I pitiless.
Speak to my father; he esteems you high.   70
I am only his; if he shall not deny

| | That equal suit, I know not what should want.
            [*aside*] Beshrew my tongue, how ready 'tis to grant.
            [*to* LUCIUS] You might in time prevail, sir, only
              so.

Gisbert   [*apart*] No word so hard in a maid's mouth as 'No'.

Lucius   Oh, let me stay thee yet to crown this hour
            With styles of happiness and by it place
            In memory this curse: if ever I embrace
            Another love, if ever I forget
            The pity shown me in distress, then let   80
            My fate run backward, let no good attend
            My present being, other than in the end
            To make my misery greater. May I obtain
            Contempt from thence where most I do affect.

Gisbert   [*Comes forward*] Thou art to blame to make such
              deep protests;
            I'll be thy gage unto my daughter – Say, Urania,
            Wilt take my word? Believe it, girl, he loves thee.
            If he prove false, lay all the blame on me.

Lucius   You oppress me, sir, with this high courtesy.
            Is't not sufficient that you gave relief   90
            Unto my fainting life when, torn with grief,
            My sad fate forc'd me hither, which dispossess'd
            True virtue of his crown and low depress'd
            The kingly Ferdinand, making sad way
            To the usurping tyrant who now sits
            High in the Sicilian blood? Is't not enough
            Your pity gave me being, but to add more
            Unto my feeble merit? My heart you had before
            (And beyond that I have not) which, with the

	acknowledgement	
	Of love and duty, shall be the annual rent	100
	I'll make just payment of.	
Gisbert	I credit thee so well that what is mine,	
	My flocks, lodge and Urania, all is thine.	
	This day I will possess thee of them, and retire	
	My weary thoughts from covetous desire	
	Of this uncertain good, and only spend	
	My hours in thanks and prayers that, ere my end,	
	So great a good befell me. I tell thee, son,	
	I'll only be thy beadsman and return	
	On thee and thine, as payment for my board,	110
	Unnumbered blessings.	
Lucius	Alas, sir, you afford	
	Deeds beyond words, which makes me find myself	
	A bankrupt ere set up, such interest your love exacts.	

Enter COSMO, LYSIPPUS, SURDO [*and*] ALEXIS

Gisbert	I am sufficient bless'd enjoying such a son; and so, in happy time, Cosmo and Lysippus – they shall be witnesses unto the contract and my performance.	
Cosmo	[*to* SURDO] Yonder he is, boy. An thou canst put on a good face, she's thine own, boy. Let me alone to work her father.	
Surdo	I had rather you would work the daughter: I shall turn tail as soon as ever I come at her.	120
Cosmo	[*aside*] Such a bashful fool was I in my infancy. The	

boy will spoil all. [*to* SURDO] Canst not tell what
to say to her?

Surdo   I think I had best begin soundly with her: tell her I
am in good health, I thank her, and so kiss her.

Cosmo   Whoreson ass! Thou must kiss her first.

Surdo   What, afore I am in good health? That will show
scurvily. Pray, let me alone. [*aside*] These old men,
though they be never so weak, will be doing in the   130
marriage business still.

Lysippus   [*to* ALEXIS] Take courage, boy, my tongue shall
   plead thy smart:
Love were no god, should he not crown desert
And just affection. [*to* GISBERT *and* URANIA]
          The happiness of the day
Befall to Gisbert and his lovely daughter.

Gisbert   The like to good Lysippus; your company is rare,
sir. You're welcome both.

Lysippus   I have a suit to you concerns me near.

Gisbert   You are happy, then, for you are like to speed.

Lysippus   Your daughter saying so, I were indeed.   140
Behold the miserablest youth that ever Love
Made captive yet, whose sight alone would move
The hungry lioness to leave her prey
And turn compassionate. If pity e'er bore sway
Within a female breast, now let it speak
And cure the wound, made by those beauteous
   eyes,

	Which pierc'd his tender heart. In you it lies To make me fatherless or happy.	
Gisbert	I would it did: thy griefs were at an end then.	
Cosmo	[*aside*] This strikes me dead. Know, Gisbert, that the same desire moves him Has brought me hither. Your land adjoins to mine, For which much suit has passed. Make but my son Your daughter's husband, both our states are one, And my death gives him all.	150
Surdo	He's half rotten already, sir. Besides the chincough, the usurer's disease, the gout and the heart-burning, the physicians have given him over long since because his feeling's gone.	
Lysippus	I have no lands to give; my flocks are all – Which were they more, are his. Think of his love.	160
Cosmo	My wealth will last when his vain passion's spent. 'Tis only riches gives thee true content.	
Gisbert	Contend no further. To cut off tedious hopes, Know you this day I have assur'd my daughter Unto Lysander.	
Cosmo and Lysippus	Your servant?	
Alexis	Unequal heaven!	
Surdo	Unequal hell, I say: this answer has brought me low enough, I'm sure.	

Urania	Content thyself, Alexis: this is the wise man's cure – That anything which Fate wills he can endure.	170
Alexis	Nay, I must bear't, and though Fate cross my will To enjoy thy person, yet I love thee still.	
Surdo	Her husband will not thank you for that! All that I can promise is this: though I cannot dance where I would, I'll shake my heels at your wedding.	
Gisbert	You shall be liberally welcome; next morrow is the day. In the mean time, I'll pass o'er my lands. 　　　　　[GISBERT] *whispers* [*to*] LUCIUS	
Cosmo	[*aside*] – which should be mine, had I my wishes. [*to* GISBERT] Farewell. - Come, boy.	
Gisbert	Nay, we'll entreat you stay a while. Come, let's in. From this day, to expect my happiness I'll begin. 　　　　　　　　　　　　　　*Exit*	180
Alexis	And I my sorrows. 　　　　　　　　　　　　*Exeunt*	

1[.2]

Enter OSWELL [*in arms*]. *Alarum.*

[*Shouts*] *within*	A Ferdinand! A Ferdinand!

Oswell	A clap of thunder stay the clam'rous throats Of this rude multitude, these virginal jacks, That skip and make a noise as each hand moves them!

Enter two LORDS

1 Lord	Oh, fly and save your life, my lord: the day is lost!
2 Lord	Our treacherous troops, making with Ferdinand, Turn head against your force, to whom the lords Joining themselves, once more proclaim him king And give free oath for their fidelity. Be rul'd and fly! The forests near will stop their pursuit. 10
Oswell	Some dismal planet strike you ever mute! You will not second me?
Both Lords	'Twere bootless.
Oswell	I won't curse you: but may you die like peasants, Slaves and cowards; and since there is no remedy But I must survive, Fortune, in spite of thee, Since not 'mongst men, a king o'er beasts I'll be. *Exeunt*

Enter FERDINAND, VINCENTIO *with a crown,*
[and] LORDS. *A flourish.*

Ferdinand	Take hence that crown: it was not sovereignty, But to release you from the tyranny Of my usurping nephew, made me leave My long-retir'd life and throw my fate 20

	Into the doubtful scale of war which, to make good,
	Know that, by solemn oath, I have tied myself
	Never to gird these temples with a crown.
All	Forbid it, heaven!
Ferdinand	Let this express your loves: you will not move me
	Beyond my vow. Yet, that we may not leave you joyless,
	We have a son: what want is in his youth,
	Your best experient wisdoms will supply.
	Make him your king. Besides his right in us,
	I have procur'd the heir of Sicily (our adjoining friend)
	To be his wife. But why with such sad brows
	And silent gestures do you take our wishes?
Vincentio	Alas, my lord! Your son –
Ferdinand	What makes this sad apostrophe?
	My heart misgives me; if my son be dead,
	Our hopes and joys with him are buried.
	Speak. Doth he live?
Vincentio	He lives, but –
Ferdinand	But what?
Vincentio	Alas, he's not himself.
	Whether his grief – depriv'd of all his friends,
	Driven to obscurity and forc'd to live
	Beneath condition of a subject, born a prince –
	Or some just fate for our ingrate offence –
	To rob us of so rich a hope as he did promise

	In his fair lineaments – is all unknown,	
	Whilst he that should be ours is not his own,	
	O'ercome with strange distraction.	
Ferdinand	Distraction is the soul of woe.	
	Poor boy! Could not thy father undergo	
	The weight of misery without thy help?	
	Oh, let me see him yet and, if his heart	50
	Give the least life unto his faculties	
	Of sense and knowledge, with arguments and prayers	
	I will recall his soul that, overpress'd	
	With melancholy blood, is barr'd her active use:	
	Like fire suppress'd, for want of heat and flame,	
	Turns to a choking vapour. It may be our presence	
	May give his flame free vent and make more light	
	That gross and earthy load.	
Vincentio	I wish it might.	
	Fortune did never envy Nature more	
	Than in so rich a cabinet to lock so poor	60
	And undervalued spirit. See where he comes!	
	Your violent passion much may wrong him, sir.	

Enter SIGISMOND *and* CATZO

Ferdinand	Unhappy Ferdinand! Beyond this cross,	
	Thou well might'st dare thy fate.	
Sigismond	Not a step lower – I am in hell already.	
Catzo	If you move him any further, he'll turn devil, claw you horribly; he'll give you his recognizance – the paw, nails and all.	

Sigismond	More weight on this side, I shall overturn else. Dost thou not see how heavy he hangs here?	70
Catzo	Thou art a crooked piece; here's more weight.	
Sigismond	One hundred pound more and I go right.	
Catzo	Half the money would make many a lord in Thessaly go wrong. Are you well now?	
Sigismond	I am reasonable well.	
Catzo	An you were reasonable well, that were well indeed. I have a mad hand with you, I am sure.	
Ferdinand	I want a language to express my grief. Poor Sigismond, I could dissolve in tears To make a passage to thy pent-up soul. If thou hast any sense, look mildly on me. Why dost thou, all in fear and terror, gaze Upon thy father thus?	80
Sigismond	Help! Help! Help!	
Catzo	Here, here, what's the matter?	
Sigismond	Has he not eat my bowels out already?	
Catzo	Who do you mean, sir?	
Sigismond	Yonder hyena.	
Catzo	Yonder hence?	

Sigismond	Dost thou not see his tears? See how cunningly he would seize me in his paw. See how he follows me. Shoot, shoot, I say! 90
Catzo	My powder's damp; it will not off.
Ferdinand	Some god or good man help!
Sigismond	He comes, he comes, he comes! Fly, fly, fly! [*Exit*]
Ferdinand	Can none prescribe me comfort?
Vincentio	May be some music would allay his passions.
Catzo	Please him with music? You may as well catch a hare with a tabor: the very tuning of the fiddles would make him stark mad.
Ferdinand	Art thou acquainted with his humours, then?
Catzo	Who? I, sir? I have almost lost mine own wits in his 100 service. 'Humours' call you them? I'll tell you, sir, sometimes he will be dumb two hours together, and then must I be speechless as long; then do we two sit, making of faces one at another like a brace of baboons or a picture-drawer at his counterfeit. Anon, he will start up and make way with his hands for fear you should run a tilt against his nose which (as he is persuaded) hangs two fathoms, in his light, at least. If anybody looks on him, he takes it in snuff and rails at him like a copper-smith; then 110 must I turn physician and make him believe I pare away two stones at least in collops.

Ferdinand	Didst ever hear him speak of his parentage, Talk of his father?
Catzo	Oh, sir! It's a tragedy if he name his father once; 'tis no boot for me to stay by it.
Ferdinand	I prithee, why?
Catzo	He says they took his crown from him and banish'd him, and then he falls upon me in his father's right and so mauls me that I am not able to lift up mine 120 hand to mine own crown. I have lost much blood in your quarrel, sir.
Ferdinand	[*to* SIGISMOND] Poor boy! It was our loss depriv'd thy sense Of her best residence and me eternally Of joy and comfort. Here, friend, [*Gives* CATZO *gold*] we will reward thee better, If thou wilt follow him still.
Catzo	Should he run out of his wits never so far, here be they would drive me after him; 'tis for these the whole world runs mad nowadays.
Ferdinand	I prithee, leave him not till we, 130 By art and good men's prayers, find out Some means to cure him. *Exit* [CATZO] Yet, that we may not seem all buried In our own particular grief, and to The commons' good ingrateful, know we confirm Your ancient privilege of senators

	Who may determine the affairs of state.
	Next, be it proclaimed that whosoever stand
	Banish'd in our cause shall be restor'd
	To honour and indued with our best love. 140
Vincentio	What death shall we inflict upon those traitors
	Ta'en in the field upon the tyrant's part?
Ferdinand	Release them freely.
	This is the difference 'twixt bad kings and good:
	The one through peace doth prosper, th'other with blood.
	Proclaim our general pardon: kings oft do grant
	That happiness to others which themselves do want.
	Let each brow put on joy, we'll only mourn;
	Our good is yours, our grief shall be our own.
	Flourish. Exeunt

1[.3]

Enter URANIA *as a bride,* GISBERT, LUCIUS, COSMO, LYSIPPUS, ALEXIS [*and*] SURDO.
Dance

Gisbert	Be this the saddest day you e'er may know!
	If ever Hymen tied a happy knot,
	Or that a parent's blessing e'er procur'd
	A good from heaven, this day a father's prayers
	Be powerful in your joys.
Lucius	Our love and duty shall deserve your wishes.
Gisbert	We cannot doubt it. Each man unto his seat.

The neighbouring shepherds, to express their love
Borne to my daughter and to grace the day
With harmless sports, are making to our lodge.   10
                              [*Music*]
These notes proclaim them.

  [*Enter* SHEPHERDS]. *Music and a dance, which
    ended, enter* MENALCAS.

          What news, Menalcas?

Menalcas A post from court, scouring along the plains,
enquir'd thy lodge and, hearing that my service
belong'd to you, charg'd me on my allegiance
deliver this proclamation that with instant speed it
might be published. [*Gives it to* GISBERT]

Gisbert [*aside*] My blood turns cold. I pray heaven all be well
         [*Reads the proclamation*]

Lucius Did he exchange no other words with thee?

Menalcas His haste denied much talk: only in brief he told me
that King Ferdinand, by the aid of the Sicilian prince,   20
was re-enthron'd; the tyrant fled; and those that erst
bewail'd their exile fortunes are again restor'd.

Gisbert This proclamation speaks it, which doth by name
give note to [*reading*] 'Lord Vincentio, late senator
of state, Francisco, Ipinolo, Jacomo – '

Lucius [*aside*] Not my name mentioned?

Gisbert 'Lord Lucius –'

Lucius	[*aside*] The same; I thought he had forgotten me.
Gisbert	'– with all other lords, knights or gentlemen that have willingly for our love or forcibly been constrained to suffer banishment, be forthwith restored with double interest for all their losses, as well in goods as rents, to be received at our Exchequer upon demand thereof made.' Most worthy Prince!
Lucius	His gratitude best speaks him.

Gisbert	And this proclamation doth confirm it, which craves my haste. Neighbours, you must along with me – all fears are past; This doubles our present joys, but time doth call – A tyrant's death makes a true festival.
	    Exeunt [GISBERT, MENALCAS, COSMO,
	      LYSIPPUS, SURDO *and* ALEXIS].

Lucius	[*aside*] This news transports me! Ferdinand restor'd, Which calls me home and adds unto my name The honour of my ancestors. Heaven cannot give A good equal to this – but I forget myself; This is my wedding day, my wife the daughter To a poor shepherd. Disgrace unto mine honour And perpetual shame to my posterity!
Urania	[*aside*] This news hath much distemper'd him. [*to* LUCIUS] Tell me, love, What means this sudden pale that doth possess Thine eyes with fear? This happy day invites All mirth and triumph; you have not now a thought

	That can give colour unto discontent.
Lucius	Forbear, you are troublesome: your words trouble me.
Urania	How? Trouble you? You speak not like a lover.
Lucius	I would I did not. Prithee, Urania, leave me.
Urania	[*aside*] Some old renewed grief possesseth him. Whate'er it be, let me bear equal part; It is my due and duty. I have a heart Beyond my sex to endure calamity. 60 [*Moves to comfort him*]
Lucius	You will offend.
Urania	Rather my soul than thee.
Lucius	Away then, get you in.
Urania	To death, shouldst thou command. - Grief-pressed heart, this day thy tears back keep. Thou'lt find hereafter time enough to weep. [*Exit*]
Lucius	She's virtuous and fair – why should I leave her, then? Her birth is low – that's Fortune's fault, not hers. Besides, she is my wife; I have married her And shall I leave her now? There is a thing Call'd Conscience would pursue me. Dull and abject thought! You fit Lysander, a poor shepherd's soul, 70 Not Lucius, son unto a senator.

              I cannot stoop so low. No, I'll abjure her sight,
              Sell both my lodge and flock to furnish me
              As is my breeding. Suppose old Gisbert curse,
              His daughter rail, talk of ingratitude?
              They beat the air. Great men are above their crimes;
              Who has a thriving soul must change with times.
              But for a chapman, let me see – Cosmo.
              His hate to Gisbert will embrace the bargain.

                         Enter COSMO [*and*] SURDO

Surdo   Father, I must leave you and return to the bride-   80
               house again.

Cosmo   Is there more to be done yet?

Surdo   It would be ill for the bride else! I must lend a hand
               to untruss her husband. He is a great lubber; he
               must to hose go down there – and see where he
               walks to keep himself in breath for the attempt.

Lucius   Cosmo – the man my thoughts direct me to.
               One word with you.
                         [LUCIUS *and* COSMO *withdraw together*]

Surdo   Now will he ask him some bawdy question or
               another, as how to get such a chopping boy as I am   90
               (bless the example) or, being now to set up, what
               course is best to maintain a standing-table. For his
               wife comes of a free stock and will keep open
               house.

Cosmo   You make but trial of me, sir.

Lucius	By all my hopes, they are thine. Give me the crowns and here is the deed.	
Cosmo	Beyond my expectation! Three hundred crowns? There they be, sir. [*Gives him the money*]	
Lucius	The flock and lodge are thine. [*Gives him the deed*] Take instantly possession.	100
Cosmo	Do you not crave this night's forbearance?	
Lucius	Not an hour, sir. Necessity will make them Ply their work, not follow me.	
Cosmo	[*aside*] I am ravish'd with the thought on't. My imagination's lost me. Gisbert's lands are mine; there's naught so sweet, As when revenge and thrifty profit meet. *Exit*	
Surdo	[*aside*] The old knave commits sin with himself. The flock and lodge gone already? I think he means to keep open house in earnest.	110
Lucius	[*aside*] This peasant's service may much pleasure me. Canst thou be secret, Surdo?	
Surdo	As a court midwife – no bawd like me.	
Lucius	Then know, I am a lord.	
Surdo	[*aside*] And that may be, indeed, for he's sold all.	
Lucius	Take but thy fortunes with me and I'll raise thee. Say, wilt along with me?	

Surdo	Will you swear by your honour you are a lord?	
Lucius	My father was no less: a senator,	120
	And, by the edict of the restored king,	
	That honour's mine. Thou shalt be next about me.	
Surdo	Your tailor will prevent me of that. I had rather come next behind you, for great men cast their sins behind them and some bribes must needs fall to my share. Are there any wenches where you go?	
Lucius	Selected beauties, such as Art and Nature contend to make perfect.	
Surdo	Art and Nature? They commonly go together, indeed. Well, I will leave my fortunes at home and run after my destiny abroad. If you prove a lord, like a fool I may the better follow you. If you gull me like a knave, you shall follow yourself. I have been brought up long enough at home to find the way back again, that's the best on't.	130
Lucius	Never doubt it, man. Arcadia, farewell!	
	Who parts from a loath'd bed is freed from hell.	
	Exeunt	

Enter COSMO, GISBERT, URANIA [*weeping*], LYSIPPUS [*and*] ALEXIS

Gisbert	Turn'd from my home! Depriv'd of all my goods,	
	My flocks, my hopes! Thou art not honest, Cosmo.	
Lysippus	Give them but respite to provide themselves.	140

Cosmo	Not a minute.
Gisbert	Let me but speak with him; I am content he shall sell all.
Cosmo	You may go seek him: you have little else To spend your time about. We were too mean To match with your fair daughter, your wealthy heir – You have advanc'd her now!
Alexis	You are too bitter, Cosmo, too pitiless: Tis baseness' self to trample on distress.
Cosmo	You may relieve them, sir, they us'd you well, Were very pitiful to you; 'twill argue love 150 An that goes naked too. Give me their hates, So I go warm and clad.
Gisbert	Hard-hearted creature!
Cosmo	Beggar-slave, pack hence from my door! I'll set my dogs upon thee else, my hounds – I keep them for no other use. If long you stay I'll give you music to your nuptial day. *Exit*
Lysippus	Unmanly wretch!
Alexis	Inhuman monster!
Urania	My heart, I think, would break Did not mine eyes, instead of words, thus speak.

Gisbert	Ingrate Lysander! Happy wert thou that curedst	160
	The wounded lion, thou Roman captive.	
	He did acknowledge thee in thy distress	
	And sav'd thy life, yet was he reasonless,	
	Had not the faculties of soul to apply	
	The good of pity to him. My poor Urania!	
	Unhappy child! 'Tis her grief wounds me more	
	Than any sorrow my spent age can know.	
Urania	Alas, I am young, sir, able to undergo	
	The worst of misery. 'Tis not my loss	
	But your tears make me weep. Pray try me, sir:	170
	Do not you mourn and see with what heart I'll bear	
	Your woes and mine – I'll not so much as weep;	
	Unless, by chance, I hear Lysander nam'd	
	And then for your sake, not mine own, I'll blame	
	His much unkindness. I'll say you us'd him better:	
	That shall be all my plaint, sir, credit me.	
Gisbert	Poor girl! How well thou mock'st calamity.	
Alexis	[*aside*] Never did grief look with a lovelier face.	
	I could e'en court it now and hold the maxim	
	'Man is not happy but in misery'.	180
	[*to* URANIA] Thou all of virtue, though my fate deny	
	The bless'd enjoying thee, make me thus proud	
	To give thy wants relief: our homely cottage,	
	My flocks and lambs are thine.	
Lysippus	Both his and mine	
	Shall pay the duty, by my best hopes I swear,	
	Or may my younglings pine, my ewes ne'er bear.	

Gisbert	We give you credit.
Alexis	Accept them, fair one.
Urania	I am more wounded with this courtesy,
	Than all Lysander's malice.
Gisbert	Thou shall accept their boons, Urania. As for me, 190
	I have another part to play: a tragedy,
	Where Justice shall rip up the heart of Cosmo
	And lay his treachery open. I'll to the court.
	[*to* LYSIPPUS *and* ALEXIS] If, until my return, you will support
	My hapless daughter's state –
Both	Make it not questionable.
Gisbert	[*to* URANIA] Nay, do not weep. Here's my hand –
	I'll not stay long from thee.
Urania	[*aside*] You must not seek me here, then. No, Lysander,
	Where'er thou art, I will or find thee out
	Or lose myself; thy sight at least I'll have. 200
	Since not thy wife, may I but live thy slave.
Lysippus	We'll bring you on your way, sir.
Gisbert	Your loves oppress me. Come, my daughter, yet
	We may, ere death, in joy each other meet.
Urania	[*aside*] Too vain a hope.
	[*to* GISBERT] Unhappy father, I'll do thee thus much right,
	Thou shalt not double sorrow by my sight. *Exeunt*

2[.1]

Thunder. Enter ADELIZIA

Adelizia Where am I? Wretched Adelizia,
What soil contains thee? You airy powers,
What further ill remains behind me
That 'mongst so many dear and worthy lives,
As has paid tribute to this fatal night,
Mine only stands exempt? Had it not been better
The sea's vast womb had given me burial
Than the unhallowed bulks of savage beasts?
And now, long wish'd-for day, what dost thou bring
But eyes to view my sorrow? Should I hap 10
To meet some passengers, 'twere to exchange
My honour with my fear, and so renew my sorrow.
Woe-curing sleep – who is only pitiful –
Would shut these casements up which do admit
But sight of grief. Then, gentle Morpheus,
I will obey thy arrest; thy leaden mace
Doth lie upon me. Down, poor, ill-starr'd maid!
                                        [*Lies down*]
Thy birth did promise better, but I see
Want best discovers idol Majesty.

Enter SIGISMOND [*and*] CATZO

Sigismond Ho! Illo, illo, illo! 20

Catzo The game's not up yet, sir. [*aside*] I think some gelder had a hand in the getting of him: he understands no language but the horn.

Sigismond I'll hunt no more, then.

Catzo	[*aside*] You'll hunt a whore, then, and that will tame you, when all is done. If a poor man had had this disease it had been whipp'd out of him, but great men may be fools or madmen and they must be humour'd forsooth. [*to* SIGISMOND] Will you go home again? [*aside*] Now he's as speechless as an unfeed attorney, not a word for the world. [*Sees* ADELIZIA] But how now? What creature's this? It should be a woman, for she lies as her mother taught her. She has the common fault of her sex: she sleeps so soundly that a man may do what he will with her. So ho! How the fool gapes! He'll ride her anon. [CATZO *shakes her*] What not move yet? What an excellent thing a woman were an she had no tongue! Hillo, illo! They say women must be roughly handled. [*Shakes her again*] She turns up the white of the eye: she should be either a punk or a Puritan by that.
Adelizia	[*Awakes*] Alas, I am betrayed! As you are men, I do conjure you –
Catzo	[*aside*] 'Las, poor soul! I thought she wanted man's help.
Adelizia	As you are virtuous, be compassionate Of a distressed maid. [*to* SIGISMOND] Fair sir, to you, My suit's to you; your eye speaks pity.
Sigismond	A fire burns within me.
Catzo	[*aside*] What a treacherous wolf's this? I cannot

	blame him: 'tis a pretty wench. If I could talk wisely, I might perchance exchange a precious stone with her.
Adelizia	Not one poor word of comfort? [*to* CATZO] Tell me, gentle friend, where am I?
Catzo	You're in a wood; yet but for one of your precious jewels and some light courtesy besides, I'll help you out.
Adelizia	If wealth will buy my freedom, you cannot ask 60 Beyond my payment. Below yon hanging rock The bodies lie of many shipwreck'd gentlemen. Yield them but burial: they'll pay thee liberal hire.
Catzo	An if they be drown'd, I may take my payment otherwise. I would be loath to take a gallant's word nowadays. Are you sure they are dead?
Adelizia	I am too sad a witness to't.
Catzo	Below yonder? [*aside*] I shall break my neck with haste to be their executor. 'Twas told me hanging or drowning would be my destiny. [*to* ADELIZIA] 70 I'll put myself in fashion and be with you presently. [*Exit*]
Sigismond	She is some goddess, sure. [*Falls to his knees*]
Adelizia	What moves this stay? [*aside*] His looks congeal my blood. [*to* SIGISMOND] Why dost thou kneel? Why wring thy hands and weep?

	Thou dost not know my griefs that they should move
	Compassion in thee.
Sigismond	Rare! More yet – speak more.
Adelizia	[*aside*] Here's sure distraction.
	[*to* SIGISMOND] Oh, if thou be'st a man,
	Art capable of passion, grief and fear,
	Leave thy amazed looks and tell the cause
	Moves this strange action.
Sigismond	Art thou a woman? 80
Adelizia	Yes, a miserable woman.
Sigismond	Let me embrace thee, then,
	Thou happy anchor of my better being.
	[*Embraces her*]
Adelizia	Defend me, heaven! [*Frees herself*]
Sigismond	Why dost thou flee me, to whom thy charmed breath
	Hath given a second soul? Thy language hath exhal'd
	All clouds whose foggy mists did captivate
	My freer sense. I am thy creature, fair;
	Depriv'd of thee, I lose that vital air
	In which I only breathe. I must, I will, enjoy thee;
	I know thou madest me not now to destroy me. 90
	[*Takes hold of her*]
Adelizia	Keep thy unchaste hands off, thou barbarous creature!

Were they thy unchaste thoughts that mov'd thy lust
To speechless ecstasy? – You powers above more
  just,
Preserve my virgin flame from the pollution
Of this insensual creature. – Keep off, I say!
                              [*Struggles to free herself*]

Sigismond I would, should all the devils in hell say nay.
Let me but draw in thy delicious breath,
But touch those lips of thine –

Adelizia   Rather to death
Would I give up my life! [*Looks up*] If there be a
  power
That guards distressed chastity, oh, hear me!   100

Sigismond Didst thou but know my thoughts, thou wouldst
  not fear me.   [ADELIZIA *moves away*]
Upon my knees I do conjure thee, stay.

Adelizia To my escape some better power make way.
See, he pursues me! Some god or good man aid me!
                                                       Exit

Sigismond If not my words, let sighs and tears persuade thee.
                                                       Exit

Enter ALEXIS

Alexis Thy search is vain, Alexis. Unkind Urania,
Thy presence was too great a good for me
Long to enjoy, nor will I e'er return
But, like a banish'd man, ever inhabit
These solitary woods; depriv'd of thee,   110

	I'll fly all others, as thy love doth me.	
Adelizia within	Help, help, help!	
Alexis	What echo beats mine ears? Is there no place But sorrow finds a passage to it?	
Adelizia	Help, help!	
Alexis	It is a woman's voice. – Speak once again And gain thy freedom, whosoe'er thou art.	

Enter ADELIZIA [*and*] SIGISMOND

Adelizia	Here, here, save a poor maid's honour!	
Sigismond	Thou wrongst my just thought much: I seek for love –	
Alexis	Rather thy beastful lust, for which receive This punishment. [ALEXIS *knocks him down*] Foul monster, lie thou there!	120
Adelizia	Oh, save his life! I do conjure you, sir. [ADELIZIA *kneels*]	
Alexis	Thou art too pitiful. Rise, beauteous maid. Remove all thoughts of fear; let me persuade: I have been virtuous, though unfortunate.	
Adelizia	This, thy humanity, o'erwhelms my joy And quite confounds the power of my mind.	

Alexis	The bliss of thine own thoughts is my reward;	
	I am happy yet to guard so fair a dame.	
Catzo within	Soho! Illo, illo, illo!	130
Alexis	But hark! – the following noise of some pursuers;	
	It may be they are known by thee.	
Adelizia	'Tis not in use for Grief to have companions:	
	My woe knows no partakers.	
Alexis	I'll be thy partner, then.	
	Wilt thou give credit to my loyal breast?	
Adelizia	As unto heaven – true virtue knows no lust.	
Alexis	Follow me, then; though mean may be thy fare,	
	Content and safety may give thee ample share.	
	Exeunt [ALEXIS *and* ADELIZIA]	
Sigismond	[*Starts up*] It was a thunderbolt. [*Looks to skies*] You have the odds of me; you are above me, sure – I had maul'd you else. But where is Europa? See where she swims away upon a bull's back! My kingdom for a boat, for a mussel boat! Lay more sails on. The envious winds blow, whirl into a mountain! I'll after her. Souse, I come, I come. *Exit*	140

2.[2]

Enter MISTRESS GULLMAN [*and*] URANIA *disguised*

Gullman Your breeding, I perceive, hath been in the country, then?

Urania It has been plain and honest.

Gullman It makes no matter – now thou art a gentlewoman. My daughter's a gentlewoman and, though I say it, as good a servant's mistress as any in all Thessaly. You shall do no worse than she doth herself; nay, she shall spare it out of her own belly rather than thou shall want it. Can you handle your needle?

Urania True stitch or so. 10

Gullman You will be past that shortly; your mistress will set you a new example, and, though I say it, she has laid her hand to as many good pieces as most ladies in the kingdom. At this instant, she is about a piece of work for the lord that is with her. She'll make him a pair of hangers ere she has done.

Urania [*aside*] Beshrew her fingers! [*to* GULLMAN] What might you call his name?

Gullman His name is Lucius. This day, he is to be made a senator; has been seven years in the wars amongst 20 the Turks and killed Jove knows how many, and

	now he swears bloodily he loves none but my daughter.
Urania	[*aside*] A bloody oath indeed: my heart doth make it good. His cruelty will cost mine and an old man's blood.
Gullman	Why do you sigh so? Are you in love?
Urania	I have small cause, forsooth.
Gullman	It's an unprofitable disease indeed: it gives that to one would serve many, and those that are men of fashion, too. You shall have gallant upon gallant here, none of your thirteen-pence-halfpenny jacks. If you have grace, you may rise, for the worst here comes a-horseback.
Urania	Has my mistress more suitors than this Lucius here?
Gullman	We had weak doings else! Good shopkeepers have wares of all sorts: some for show and some for fashion. And yet, to speak truth, he doth well for both: his countenance keeps the painted staff in awe and saves us many a fair bribe. Besides, my daughter makes him come off at her pleasure, and yet it is not one wind can keep her mill a-going. One of these days she'll turn him off to thee; if thou please her well, thou mayest have him in reversion.
Urania	I should have, had I my right, but 'tis too great a happiness for me, so much unworthy. Lysander, a

| | poor shepherd, was my husband, and would he had been so still. [*aside*] Forgive me, Lucius, 'tis my love that wrongs thee. And here he comes, | 50 |

Enter LUCIUS *and* FLAVIA

and had I but mine own,
Those happy arms might 'bout my waist be thrown.

| Lucius | I know no reason for't, and yet my heart Seems to proclaim some sadness. I would This day were o'er. |

| Flavia | I could be more merry now, and yet I have had a heavy night on't, too. |

| Urania | [*aside*] Would I had eas'd you of your burden. |

| Flavia | How melancholy you are, sir! I believe you have another love. Hi ho – the very thought of it! | 60 |

| Lucius | I prithee do not wrong my faith so much. By my hopes, till I beheld thy face, I knew not what love was – by this, I did not. [*Kisses her*] |

| Urania | [*aside*] Thou art perjur'd then, and yet thy vow's nothing; 'Tis a false book thou tak'st thine oath on. |

| Gullman | 'Tis early morning, sir, walk one turn more in the backside – stirring will get you a stomach. [*to* FLAVIA] Do you begin to weep already? We shall |

THE POOR MAN'S COMFORT 39

	have a day on't then. [*to* LUCIUS] No sooner is your back turned, but here is sigh upon sigh; her heart goes in her pulses and beats pit-a-pat, pit-a-pat, till the tears trickle down again. Never was young gentlewoman so overborne with affection. Heaven give her good on't! If you should leave her in the suds now –
Lucius	Time shall be false to truth first! Come, I shall be angry with you. Come, prithee smile upon me, love. [*Kisses* FLAVIA]
Urania	[*aside*] I could shed tears might they be so ta'en off.
	Enter SURDO
Surdo	So ho! Mistress Gullman, I have been knocking below till my heart ache. Where is my lord?
Lucius	Your business, sir?
Surdo	My business? Nay, that's done, sir. The senate has stayed for you any time this half hour.
Flavia	[*to* SURDO] Thou wrong'st me, friend, to rob me of my love. Sweet Lucius, thou shalt not part from me.
Lucius	My honour doth enforce me to it. By this diamond, [*Gives it to her*] I will not stay a minute longer than necessity constrains me.
Gullman	This gentleman protests most nakedly; upon such an oath I'll believe any man.

(Line numbers: 70, 80, 90)

Surdo	[*to* GULLMAN] By this French crown, I'll be with that new gentlewoman. [*Shows her the money*] Will you believe me now?
Gullman	I'll talk with you upon the premises.
Surdo	[*aside*] This is the arrantest bawd in Christendom! My master, like a gull, lies tiring upon a ringtail, whilst I am at variety of fresh, tame fowl. 'Tis the bravest life! Since I turn'd courtier, I do nothing but drink, whore and sleep. [*to* LUCIUS] Will you be going, sir? 100
Flavia	You shall hear her sing first – in troth, you shall.
Lucius	Have you a good voice, Castadora?
Urania	A sad voice, sir.
Flavia	I'll ha' you sing a merry song: 'I am a maid and I cannot mend it'.
Urania	I have no variety: I can sing but one song.
Lucius	Let's have that. What's the subject?
Urania	'Tis of a hapless shepherdess, forsaken by her false lover. 110
Lucius	'Tis too sad. I do not like it.
Urania	[*aside*] I would you did not: I might sing merrily then.

Surdo	[*aside*] This wench has been with a conjurer, I hold my life. She knows all my lord's knavery.
Lucius	This day is ominous, I fear. [*to* FLAVIA] Farewell, till night we part; No hell but in an absent lover's heart. *Exit*
Urania	[*aside*] That proves thy cruelty, That sufferest mine so long in hell to be. 120
Gullman	[*to* SURDO] Cannot you persuade him?
Surdo	He's troubled with the great man's ill – cannot endure to hear of his faults. You'll remember me; I have left a familiar token with you – the French thing you wot on.
Gullman	Be confident. *Exit* [SURDO] Is he gone?
Flavia	Hang him, gull! I am as weary of him as of a fever.

Enter JASPERO

	But see, here comes Jaspero, my dearest lover.
Urania	[*aside*] Monster of women! 130
Jaspero	I cannot stay with you, beauty; I only come to give you the maidenhead of my new clothes. You are for the show?
Flavia	The new upstart lord would ha' provided me a

	standing, but I took an order with him before he went.
Gullman	We can ha' standings there without his providing. I ha' been put in, ere now, in the lobby, when my betters have stood bare before me, and have had many a sweet bit out of the pastery and out of the pantry, too. They are as kind men – 140
Jaspero	I believe, madam. You are welcome. [*Sees* URANIA] Fair, what gentlewoman's this?
Gullman	A poor virgin wants help, heaven send it her!
Jaspero	[*to* FLAVIA] When shall's come to the breaking-up of this giblet pie? When will thy love be out of the way?
Flavia	Hang him, hornpipe! A small mist puts out his eyes. When you will.
Gullman	Though he should see, what cannot we persuade? 150 Man was asleep when woman's brain was made. 　　　*Exeunt* [GULLMAN, FLAVIA *and* JASPERO]
Urania	Immodest strains of womanhood! Did ever Poor creature fall upon so hard fortune? What misery can belong to her hath seen Her aged father turn'd to beggary, Laden with contempt, his silver hairs press'd down With the same weight? Life, I am weary of thee; I'll flatter thee no longer. My Lucius' hand Shall force thee from me. If he deny this good – By violent hand to shed my hated blood – 160

2[.3]

Enter GISBERT

Gisbert This is the court, sure, whose eminence proclaims
Fair Justice's seat is here, who sits on high
That no man suspect partiality.
Here, in rich purple clad, her followers go:
Each man for his desert and not for show.
The oppressed poor man's advocates, whose unfeed tongues
Turn willing orators, retort the wrongs
Upon the oppressor's head. Cosmo shall find
Though bribing sorcerers picture Justice blind,
She has eyes to see his cruelty. He shall perceive   10
Poor men have friends, though they be far off.
I'll leave a precedent behind for't. And see

Enter JASPERO [*and*] LICURGO

Where some of them appear! I must not yet
Give interruption to them; their brains are troubled
About business of state, the kingdom's good.
Whilst others sleep secure, these spend their blood,
Out-watch the tedious night, only to gain
Titles of honour hardly worth the pain.

Jaspero I shall never sleep till I find out for which of his
good parts this Lucius was made a senator.   20

Licurgo Thou art in the high way to madness, then. Which

	of his good parts? Dost make a gentleman-usher of him?
Jaspero	I have examined myself, and my glass tells me I have as simple a chin, speak as few languages, can wear perfum'd boots and beggar my tailor, keep a whore, be lousy, be as impudent, jeer at that I understand not, make antic faces and lie as damnably, all as forward –
Licurgo	Backward in the way of preferment. I'll tell thee: it may be he broke his shin and, having a good surgeon, kept not his chamber above three days and so his valour raised him; or took a box on the ear, swore he would put it up, and so his patience raised him. Some unknown virtue or other did it.
Jaspero	Nay, that's certain – but we neglect the show.
Gisbert	[*apart*] Their serious talk is ended. [*to* LICURGO] Most honoured sir, I have a suit to you.
Jaspero	Let me have the preferring, I am your first man.
Licurgo	By this hand, I'll share with thee.- Speak it, old man.
Gisbert	[*aside*] Did not I tell you? Here are true statesmen. How they contend in virtue, even ambitious To do poor men good! [*to* JASPERO] This paper speaks my right. [*Gives him the paper*]
Licurgo	Canst read, Jaspero? A monopoly, transportation or concealment?

Gisbert	'Tis a particular grief, sir.	
Jaspero	Of some particular corporation –	
Gisbert	That lies as heavy on the bearer's shoulders.	
Licurgo	Some suit from Porters' Hall, belike not worth begging.	50
Jaspero	Beggary itself! [*Reads*] 'The petition of Gisbert and his daughter, dispossess'd of a cottage, two roods of land and a sheep-walk by the lewd practice of –'. Dost take us for justice's clerks?	
Gisbert	The friends of Justice, sir.	
Jaspero	So are they: their mistress could not share with them else. Take your humble complaining and pack hence. The porter will give you a mark to be known by – and know men of our rank a little better, else.	60
Gisbert	My cause is just and I poor. Pray, will you read my petition?	
Jaspero	We had rather thy cause were wrong and thou rich. Do we look as though we lived by relieving the poor? You whoreson gull! You shepherd!	
Licurgo	How the slave smells of tar and hog's grease! *Exeunt* [JASPERO *and* LICURGO]	
Gisbert	These are not virtuous, sure. I am mistaken: Justice has not her being here; and yet I had directions hither – I'll make a further trial.	

Enter CATZO, *gallant*

Catzo — Pray Jove the sight be not past yet! This suit will bear me out: I am in fashion from the beaver downward. I would be loath to have the repulse. 70

Gisbert — Most worthy sir —

Catzo — I know none of that name. [*aside*] If the gentleman-usher might but see my roses, it would prick him forward to my admittance.

Gisbert — How's this? A word with you. Do you know where I might find Justice?

Catzo — Justice? What's that? A man or a woman?

Gisbert — The poor man's friend, sir: she that never yet did take or give tribute. 80

Catzo — What, dost thou look for her so near the porters' lodge? Honest friend, be rul'd by me: return the way thou camest. Here's no place for such fellows.

Gisbert — Oh, hear my reply, sir!

Catzo — [*aside*] Should I be but seen to confer with a fellow of his rank, it were enough to call my wit in question, and that were simple, very simple, in sooth.   *Exit*

Gisbert — Monstrous! All man is lost in't. What an ass have I been who, all this while, have thought that which should make up perfect man had been within him. 90

How ignorant were our fathers
That spent so many tedious hours in art,
That by so many precious acts did strive,
To attain those types of honour and regard
Which now a tailor and ten yards of silk
Will throw upon a man. I can but pity them,
Silly, weak men! They, clad in russet grey,
By deeds sought titles; these have a nearer way,   100
To what? To hell! Damnation follow them!
Happy Musaeus, now I well perceive
Thou, by experienced notes, didst not in vain
Foretell the change of times when, to the plain
From these tempestuous hills, thou didst retire.
I have forgot how oft thou wouldst bemoan
Astraea's flight to heaven: that, Justice gone,
Extortion took her seat, attended on
By Pride and Ignorance. Oh, I could curse,
Dissolve to tears, yet laugh too, for this sight   110
Affordeth both. Who is't would not smile
To see an idiot proud, as garnish'd posts whose
  house
Is but a sink, mere rottenness, within?
This silly ass – what good within himself
Can make him proud? His silks are none of his;
He only bears them as a camel treasure.
Should the poor worm take from him what is hers,
How naked were he, nay, how pitiful!
Oh, 'twould distract a temperate virtue to behold
Those piebald jays sit on the eagle's perch,   120
These airy bubbles, outsides, wearing more wealth
Beneath their knees than would relieve the want
Of twenty worthier, yet distressed, souls.
Here comes another of them. Ha! If mine eyes
Deceive me not –

Enter LUCIUS [*and*] SURDO

Lucius	Now, Surdo, are all things fit?
Surdo	They are all ready, sir – your men, I mean. Marry, how fit you may imagine, considering most of them wear borrowed clothes. There was never senator, I think, had half so many attendants. 130
Lucius	Why, prithee, thy reason?
Surdo	There's never a man of yours but has a follower or two of his own for fear they should run away with their borrowed goods. You shall have them at a beck; they are watch'd for stealing.
Gisbert	[*aside*] 'Tis he, my son, Lysander! Heart, thou art oppress'd with joy! I could e'en blame my unadvised thoughts that ere were moved with loss of my estate, which, with his merit, has thus advanc'd him. Ay, he has too much virtue in him to 140 want preferment long.
Surdo	My honour'd lord, the Senate doth attend you.
Lucius	I'll instantly attend them. [*aside*] Heart! Gisbert this way?
Gisbert	Stay, worthy son. Mine eyes are drown'd in joy. 　　　　　　　　　　　[LUCIUS *tries to leave*] Lysander, stay. Old Gisbert speaks to thee.

Lucius	To me? Thou art mistaken. [*to* SURDO] Give the poor man an alms.	
Surdo	Have you any single money about you? Give me sixpence – here's a groat. [*aside*] We that carry the purse must profit by it.	150
Gisbert	Is not your name Lysander? This Surdo? Did not you marry Urania, my daughter?	
Surdo	How? He marry your daughter? Marry, faugh!	
Lucius	I wonder such are suffered to approach so near the court. [*to* SURDO] Command the officers to void him.	
Gisbert	Oh, inhuman wretch! I will pursue thee, villain.	
Lucius	Nay, then you'll be too troublesome. [*Spurns him and exits*]	
Surdo	'Foot! Have you no more wit than to think a lord will acknowledge you for his father? Were you my father, it should be upon good terms ere I would take acquaintance on you.	160
Gisbert	Leave me, you faculties of reason. Virtue, Thou art a beggar; I will hate thy company. There's none but fools and knaves that happy be. [*to* SURDO] Canst thou deny thy name? Didst not thou come from the Arcadian plains?	
Surdo	What an ass is this! We came from a bawdy-house. Stay but a little, I'll show thee the way thither.	

	We'll be very jovial; I command all the under-whores. Thou shalt go upon the ticket with her.	170
Gisbert	Insufferable! Man cannot bear it.	
Surdo	It will try your back, that's certain – marry, then you shall have your eringo roots, crab's guts, dove's pizzles, fried clary, and lamb's stones that shall –	
Gisbert	Thou wilt provoke me, slave.	
Surdo	Oh, beyond all measure! What is it makes threescore venture upon a girl of sixteen? Stay but a little till the Senate rise, and thou shalt to't, old lad. Make it not strange. If it be a sin, 'tis of a good standing, ever since Adam. I'll be for thee presently.	180
	Exit	
Gisbert	Dissolve, thou seat of life, that dost not yield One good that's worthy life – so many deaths Each hour pursue us. Thou dastard earth, Why dost thou, on thy aged shoulders, bear More sorrows yet, when as one groan would end Thy misery and ours? What ill canst thou expect Beyond this age of sin? Would'st thou behold More bribery? Dost think thou canst sustain more, More sighs of wronged innocents, whose tears Have eaten into thy bowels? Dost thou desire To bring forth more ingrateful monsters yet, Whose sights have turn'd all charity to flint? Hast thou no place of refuge left? Yes, the Senate – They will relieve thee, Gisbert. These are men Bred of superfluous humour; the sound blood Lies at the heart. Thy wrongs once understood	190

By those impartial judges, thy woes are cur'd.
They are the kingdom's props by whom secur'd
The harmless lamb lies by the ravenous wolf
And smiles to see him grin. Oh, pardon me, 200
You honourable men that sway this monarchy,
As the first Mover doth the general globe,
In equal motion. I will recant mine error
And to posterity speak your partless dooms.
For their base minds are sway'd by bribes and blood;
The world shall know great men are just and good.

Exit

3[.1]

Cornets for a dumb show.
Enter OFFICERS *with robes fitting a senator,*
LUCIUS *between* LEONARDO *and* SILLEUS;
[GLISCO, VINCENTIO *and*] *the rest attendant. Two*
OFFICERS [*remain upstage; the rest pass over the stage
and exeunt*].

[*Enter upstage a crowd of petitioners including* CATZO
and GISBERT]

1 Officer Bear back! Room for the Senate! Bear back – you are too forward. [*to* CATZO] I do not speak to you, sir. Make room for the gentleman in the embroidered doublet!

Catzo My hose are suitable to it, I assure you, sir.
[CATZO *moves downstage*]

Gisbert I beseech you, sir – my entrance much concerns me.

1 Officer What's that to me? Dost think I stand here for nothing?

Gisbert You must pardon my ignorance. Here's all I have –
[*Gives him money*]

1 Officer Nay, then, you will in, sir.   10
GISBERT [*moves downstage*]

Gisbert I swear he stands not there for nothing. The heaven of justice must needs be seated there, here is such hard entrance.

THE POOR MAN'S COMFORT

Enter LUCIUS, LEONARDO, VINCENTIO, SILLEUS [*and*] GLISCO. [*They move downstage and take their seats.* GISBERT *pushes to the front of the crowd*]

2 Officer	What means this rude companion? [*to* GISBERT] Stand back.
Gisbert	[*aside*] This officer must have somewhat, too, but I have never an asper left. I shall never be able to purchase another entrance if I do not speak.
2 Officer	This fellow dotes.
Gisbert	Not of thy company. [*Steps forward*] Justice, grave sirs, let me have justice! 20
Lucius	[*aside*] Death! Gisbert here?
Gisbert	If ever you'll deserve the prayers of good men, Or have your names preserv'd to happy memory When souls corrupted rot, give a free ear To mine inhuman wrongs.
2 Officer	Fellow, stand back.
Vincentio	Officer, forbear. Speak freely, aged man.
Lucius	[*aside*] Some planet strike him dead! [*to* SENATORS] This fellow's mad, talks of a daughter lost; Has had some hindrance by her and, being cross'd, Will rail at any man he meets. 30

Gisbert   Most shameless impudence!

Leonardo   He's far gone, indeed.
'Twere fit he had some physic given him
Or carried to the house of the *Insani*.

Silleus   His age doth make him past recovery.
Poor man! Who brought him hither?

Gisbert   [*aside*] How's this? Do they take me for a mad man?

Vincentio   I see no sign of such distemperance.
Speak, aged father; who has done thee wrong?

Gisbert   [*Pointing to* LUCIUS] That monster, Lysander, that
ingrateful wretch! 40

Silleus   Ha, ha, ha! Alas, good old man!

Vincentio   'Lysander'? Thy passion blinds thee, sure. Here's
none of that name.

Gisbert   [*to* LUCIUS] Is not your name 'Lysander'? Did
not you marry my daughter?

Lucius   [*aside to* SENATORS] I told you as much before. A
place more private (or less free of air) would fit
him better.

Leonardo   See how his eyes turn. How fearfully he gazes on
us! It is a deep lunacy. 50

Glisco   As I am a statesman, I pity him.

Gisbert	It may be I am mad, have lost my senses. I must confess, I have not been mine own man this twenty days.
Glisco	It seems no less.
Gisbert	[*to* LUCIUS] Yet, let me tell you, sir, were you Lysander – as you look very like him – I could unfold a tale that, had you hearts of flint –
Vincentio	His words, methinks, speak no distraction. Say, aged father; if thy griefs be curable, thou shalt find comfort. 60
Gisbert	Nay, it makes no matter; I shall but trouble you. I find my sorrows have o'ercome me and o'erturn'd my brain, and I'd be very loath –
Lucius	To trouble us? Poor man, go home. Thou but disturb'st thy soul with the renewing of some ancient grief.
Gisbert	[*to* SENATORS] Look on me once again and tell me if I be mad, have lost the faculties of a reasonable man, as sight or hearing.
Glisco	Lost all, as I am truly virtuous. 70
Vincentio	[*to* GLISCO] You wrong your judgement.
Gisbert	[*to* VINCENTIO] I'll be tried by you, sir, you which do seem to have some spark of man left. I'll trust your eyes: compassion speaks in them. Am I myself – a knowing creature, able to distinguish?

Vincentio	Thou art; discourage not thyself. However grief transports thee, thou art as free from lunacy as myself.
Lucius	[*aside*] Vexation!
Gisbert	Then he that sits in purple there's a villain! 80
Lucius	Now, by mine honour, I'll pluck thy tongue out!

[LUCIUS *moves to strike* GISBERT *but* SENATORS *restrain him*]

Vincentio	This violence proves some guilt.
Gisbert	Nay, let him come; has only left me life, And that I am weary of. Here, let him take it. The groaning earth, the silent air, shall speak In thundering accents my inhuman wrongs.
Vincentio	Leave circumstance; name the particulars.
Gisbert	I must give larger vent first: they have too long possess'd This narrow seat. Know, honour'd sir, this man – I cannot name him; once did bear Lysander's name, 90 But that, as all his deeds, may well be counterfeit – Some ten years since, laden with grief and sorrow, Made to my lodge – though poor, yet happier far Than those whose turrets much more lofty are. It was that day made fatal by the loss Of virtuous Ferdinand –

Lucius	[*aside*] Some planet strike him dead!	
Gisbert	His eyes and silent gesture spake his griefs.	
	No tedious way was made to his relief:	
	It was sufficient that his wants were known.	100
	True charity makes others' wants her own.	
	I gave him safe repose; no gold prevail'd,	
	Though much was offer'd to have his life betray'd.	
	What should I say? I gave him my consent	
	Unto my daughter's love. Poor maid – pardon my tears –	
	She did deserve –	
Lucius	[*to* SENATORS] You wrong your worthy ears,	
	To hear a madman thus.	
Vincentio	You wrong yourself.	
	By all my ancestors, I do suspect –	
Lucius	Your wisdom, do you not?	
Vincentio	Rather thy honesty.	
Glisco	You are too forward, Vincentio.	110
Vincentio	What? In relieving misery? Would you had no greater crimes! Father, proceed.	
Gisbert	Nay, I was almost at an end:	
	Beyond that ill Fortune cannot extend a curse.	
	I mean the saddest nuptial betwixt	
	My child and him, with whom he had all	
	And more he could not have. To express him in a word:	

	No sooner happy fate our King restor'd
	But he, ingrateful, not only left
	His too, too miserable wife but, to express 120
	The hateful soul of base ingratefulness,
	Sold both our house and flocks. Nor did he blush
	To expose those limbs to hateful beggary
	That fed and cloth'd his naked misery.
Vincentio	A tale as sad as true.
Lucius	[*to* GISBERT] Peace, howling peasant!
	My merit's known to stand above deprave
	Of such a Bedlam tongue. [*to* SENATORS] For you that please
	To sit and hear my honour scandalis'd,
	Know Time may turn his glass and give me cause
	To smile and laugh as much at you. *Exit*
Gisbert	[*to* SENATORS] Do you then fear him? 130
	If Justice's self be aw'd, no marvel, then,
	If strange oppression prey on weaker men.
Leonardo	You are too violent, old man; a while give way.
Gisbert	Most willingly. [GISBERT *draws back*]
Vincentio	To such foul crimes we may allow no favour.
Glisco	You do forget: he's high in birth and place.
Vincentio	His highness will add so much more honour
	Unto the justice of the punishment.

Leonardo	Who strikes a lion must be sure strike home	
	Lest, aiming at his life, he lose his own.	140
	Such game I like not. [*to* GISBERT] Old man, come near. [GISBERT *approaches*]	
	May I advise thee, thou shouldst leave thy suit.	
Gisbert	First, I will leave my life.	
Leonardo	Nay, since you are so peremptory, know	
	Thy accusation's idle: thou bring'st no proof.	
Gisbert	No proof?	
Leonardo	His worth is known; thy age and poverty	
	Do move thy tongue beyond a certainty.	
	Howsoever, his desert, for so mean a fact,	
	Does plead sufficient pardon were the act	150
	More capital. Men of your ranks	
	Must put up injuries and render thanks. *Exit*	
Gisbert	Good, very good!	
Silleus	He tells you true; it may be our own case.	
	Shall we, upon complaint of men so base,	
	Be questioned? No, cedars are cedars still.	
	The valley must not dare to climb the hill.	
	Poor men must suffer; rich do what they will. *Exit*	
Gisbert	Better and better!	
Glisco	I admire their judgements that with mine just aim'd,	160
	And I with them, as men bless'd in one fate.	
	Should I dissent from them I were not wise in state.	
	Exit	

Gisbert	Best of all!
Vincentio	Poor man, I pity thee but cannot help.
	Thou hadst best go home; thy sorrows make thee sad.
	The good that I can do thee is this: the world is bad.
	Exeunt [VINCENTIO *with* OFFICERS *and crowd, leaving* GISBERT *alone on stage*]
Gisbert	Have you now said? I hope you'll give me leave
	At least to answer you. [*Looks around*] Ha! All gone?
	'Tis not possible! This is the Senate House,
	The poor man's audience chamber – it cannot be. 170
	Thou shalt have justice, sure. See with what silence
	They attend thy griefs. He that erst put thee back,
	How quietly he stands to give thee passage.
	He lies that says this judgement seat's not free
	And open unto justice. Yes, Gisbert, thou shalt have justice. [*Steps forward*]
	Most worthy senators, this paper speaks my grief –
	An old man's grief, an old man's crying griefs.
	[*Mimes handing over the petition*]
	See with what greedy eyes they read it! Tush, Gisbert,
	Thou shall have right, man: Equity itself sits here.
	This place admits no favour, bribe nor fear. 180
	He ascends the state [*and acts the part of each senator*]
As Leonardo	What's here? Gisbert craves justice against a peer,
	A senator? The man's distracted sure.

As Silleus	Far gone, indeed! See how his eyes do turn.
	How fearfully he gazes on us, poor man!
	Come hither? Alas, it were more fit
	Thou wert in Bedlam, there to learn more wit.
As Glisco	As I am just, I pity him. Lead him hence.
	A shepherd sue a lord? Poor innocent,
	What mak'st with us? Thou art out of the way, sure.
	We sit here about affairs more profitable. 190
As Vincentio	But not more just. Now, by my blood,
	You wrong the man. 'Tis not distemperance
	But grief that moves his tongue. His cause is just
	And he shall find –
As Leonardo	Your weakness, shall he not?
	Do you forget he's low and base, his adversary great?
	– Old man, be rul'd by me and leave us.
	Yet, if thou needs wilt stay, know this:
	Thy accusations were they ne'er so true,
	We must respect his eminence, not you.
	Poor men are born to wrongs, low are their ranks; 200
	The more they are trod upon, the more they must give thanks.
As Silleus	He tells you true; it may be our own case.
	Should one great thief condemn another? It were base.
	Let them steal on; cedars are cedars still.
	Poor men must suffer; rich do what they will.
As Glisco	I admire thy wisdom that with mine just aim'd,
	And I with them, as men bless'd in one fate.
	Should I dissent from them I were not wise in state.

As Vincentio	Poor man, I pity thee but cannot help.	
	Thou hadst best go home, or stay here and run mad.	210
	The good that I can do thee is this: the world is bad.	
[*Gisbert as himself*]	You empty-pated judges, painted idols,	
	Whose souls are purpler than the robes you wear;	
	Whose ear's more deaf unto the poor man's cries	
	Than Hell's to pity; I will go home,	
	And every step my soul shall utter a curse	
	Which, meeting with the repercussive earth,	
	Shall beat yon marble vault and wake the gods	
	Who, with a leaden hand, hold justice back	
	From falling on the impious heads of men;	220
	And when mine fails, Urania's tongue shall help –	
	Lysander's name will make her eloquent	
	In exclamations. The day thus spent,	
	With jealousy we'll watch the wanton night.	
	No sooner shall a star dart forth his light	
	Through her ebon veil but from our eyes	
	A downy vapour, like a mist, shall rise	
	To choke his fires and fright the partial watch.	
	The day we'll spend in curses; the night we'll weep	
	Till tears glue down our eyes to mock sad sleep.	230
	Exit	

3[.2]

Enter FERDINAND, LICURGO, VINCENTIO[, GLISCO *and attendants*]

Ferdinand	Move us no more. Having seen the fort and taken order for those soldiers, we'll choose a wife for Lucius to equal him in birth, and place him as our

THE POOR MAN'S COMFORT 63

lieutenant over them. Till this be done, we'll take
no sleep. *Horn within*

Enter POST [*who gives letters to* FERDINAND]

How now? From whence these letters?

Post	From Sicily.
Ferdinand	How fares your King Valerio?
Post	In perfect health. These letters crave perusal with all speed.
Ferdinand	Our leisure serves us not. Till soon, Vincentio, we'll defer the reading of them; and with the morning sun let our secretary dispatch him with an answer.
Post	I do beseech your Majesty –
Ferdinand	Be not so importunate. Forbear till morn. *Exit*
Post	'Tis news I fear, though late, will come too soon. [*Exeunt*]

10

3[.3]

Enter SIGISMOND [*and*] CATZO

Catzo   [*aside*] What a mad gentleman's this? Whither will
he lead me?

Sigismond	I take it you are a magician can blind men's eyes with apparitions and turn yourself into diverse strange shapes and proportions.
Catzo	[*aside*] Who told him of my purpose, trow?
Sigismond	I will put you to your purgations, sir. I will have you show me a sort of virgins, about the age of twenty, honest.
Catzo	'Tis impossible. Art cannot find them out, I assure you.
Sigismond	I will have them poor, too. Then, thou shalt find me twenty honest lawyers that are rich.
Catzo	They are not in nature, neither.
Sigismond	And they shall marry with those virgins, and so we may chance to have an honest breed of them. I am a good commonwealth's man; I will have it so – do not defer it. Art not a conjurer?
Catzo	A poor scholar, sir, and that's next door to beggary; they are cousin-germanes.
Sigismond	I am mistaken: thou art a philosopher. Pick me a salad for my dinner and by that time I'll be with you in philosophy.
Catzo	Pick you a salad? I had as lief pick rushes. I cannot tell how to pick a salad, not I.

Enter GISBERT

	Who comes here? Another madman? Hell's broke loose, sure! I were best to run away.	
Gisbert	[*apart, looking at his petition*] 'Tis done in dismal characters. How black it looks – especially towards the latter end where they did make away my daughter. Now, let me see, what shape would fit me best?	30
Catzo	[*aside*] An ass's shape, if your advocate hath left you worth your ears.	
Gisbert	[*apart*] Rare! I ha't – into a night raven's: it will suit with my revenge. For when the evening grows late, these prying statesmen sit in their closets, plotting some innocent's fall which to their net may bring a golden draught. My wings shall beat their casements open and, with horrid clamours and croaks, affright their guilty souls. Oh, 'twill be rare to see those made others, make themselves despair!	40
Sigismond	[*to* CATZO] Do ye hear, sir? Before we enter into disputation, I'll put a case of state upon you. I know you are a politician.	
Gisbert	[*to* SIGISMOND] A word with you, sir. Is this a senator?	
Sigismond	Dost make a doubt on't? Is he not cloth'd in purple? Shalt hear him give his charge. Grave father, take your seat.	50
Catzo	This world will not last long, sure: learning is so	

	suddenly advanced. [CATZO *sits*]
Sigismond	[*to* GISBERT] Now, sir, have you any business with this learned man?
Gisbert	Special business! [*to* CATZO] Does not your lordship know Gisbert?
Catzo	That name is known to me.
Gisbert	And his daughter's too, is't not?
Catzo	He had a daughter.
Gisbert	But thou hast murdered her! 60

[GISBERT] *plucks* [CATZO] *down* [*from his seat and throws him to the ground*]

Sigismond	Oh, save the physician! Learning's overthrown else!
Catzo	Hold, sir, hold! I am no senator; I am a foolosopher.
Gisbert	A philosopher? Then rise, Aristarchus.
Catzo	[*Gets up*] You have made a stark ass of me, I am sure.
Gisbert	[*to* SIGISMOND] Are you a philosopher, too?
Sigismond	Keep off! I shall break in pieces else; I am made all of glass. Canst thou not see quite through me?
Gisbert	[*to* SIGISMOND] I took him for a senator, a man

	of state, those we call great ones.	70
Catzo	You have made a little one of me. I might have kept me out of your claws, like a coxcomb as I was, if I had known you would ha' played horse-play with me.	
Gisbert	[*to* CATZO] But since you are a philosopher, I'll put you to your books.	
Catzo	Not I, sir. I was put to that afore and, since it will not save me, I'll be hang'd ere I trust to't any more. There's a gentleman of your own humours [*pointing to* SIGISMOND]; he'll dispute like a puritan – without all sense or reason.	80
Gisbert	Then this learned man shall be moderator. [*to* SIGISMOND] Nay, sit down. If you prove not a philosopher, I'll make an ass of you presently.	
Sigismond	I would be loath to crack – the least touch makes a flaw in me. [SIGISMOND *sits*]	
Gisbert	[*to* CATZO] Thus, I oppose you, philosopher: if justice be *corpus simplex,* a 'simple body,' as philosophy defines it, how comes it that she desires composition and deals not simply, according to her nature, without a working element be join'd with her?	90
Catzo	This question's able to put ten constables and their bills to silence – yet I'll answer you, sir. Justice is a simple body. Now, sir, the more simple the body is, the better clothing it requires, and great reason –	

	for the most part, she wears loose garments, and now, being to cut her coat out of a broad cloth, she had not need of slender comings-in, sir.	
Sigismond	But Justice is blind, sir!	100
Catzo	True, sir, and therefore subject to go astray; and therefore she had need have the more help to put her in the way.	
Gisbert	I'll have another bout with you, philosopher.	
Catzo	A few more bouts will make me turn fencer and run away – 'tis the safest ward, when all is done.	
Gisbert	Have at you, sir! Thus I oppose you, Master Philosopher: if heavy bodies that are composed of earth descend downward, how comes it that so many fools and usurers rise upward?	110
Catzo	[*aside*] As I am an honest man, I shall never be able to answer him.	
Gisbert	I ha' put you to't; make no demurs lest I join issue with you. [*Pulls up his sleeves as if to fight*]	
Catzo	Hold, hold! [*aside*] He'll beat that into me which he wants himself.	
Gisbert	Are you ready?	
Catzo	You are, I am sure, else; but I'll answer you. The reason that fools and usurers rise upward is this: Fortune's a whore. Now, your whore is a light	120

	creature, you know, and of herself turns upward. Now this whore, doting upon none but fools and usurers, with a violent hand bears them along with her.
Gisbert	Why had not this whore, Fortune, been carted, then?
Catzo	Because she has the usurer to her friend and buys it out, sir.
Gisbert	Let me embrace thee, most wise Lucullus. 　　　　　　　[*Embraces* CATZO] Give Learning place.
	[GISBERT *pushes* SIGISMOND *off his seat. He falls to the ground*]
Catzo	Alas, you ha' beat out his bottom! Did he not tell you he was all glass? We shall never joint him together again.
Sigismond	I find myself in two. Hold, or I shall fall in pieces!
Gisbert	What bad fortune had I to break so rare a piece of workmanship!
	Enter FERDINAND [*holding letters*], VINCENTIO, GLISCO, [LICURGO *and* OFFICERS]
Ferdinand	Fair Adelizia shipwreck'd? Let each eye, drown'd in tears, Participate her loss. Command throughout our land An universal day of sorrow. Hapless maid,

130 appears at line "Alas, you ha' beat out his bottom!..."

	Not thine but my impartial fate had sway
	In thy untimely obit. Behold him that confirms it: 140
	My all of grief and joy! [*to* SIGISMOND] Poor boy, could I
	Recover, with my life's loss, thy well-being –
	But thou art all incurable.
Sigismond	True, Aesculapius; I am.
Catzo	You must bear with him: he is no wiser than he should be. He thinks he is glass and with this fall broke in a thousand pieces.
Ferdinand	Let him into our palace. Henceforth, we'll not expose him
	To experiment of art; ourself will be his keeper.
	His sight, at least, will do a true friend's part 150
	And banish flattering comfort from my heart.
	[*Sees* GISBERT] What aged man is that in whom grief looks
	So pale? It makes us fearful to behold him.
Gisbert	[*aside*] It is the king of birds, sure. How all crouch to him and do him willing homage!
Ferdinand	Speak. What art thou?
Gisbert	Though old, dread sovereign, yet vouchsafe him hearing
	Will lay such black deeds ope will banish night
	Forever from her veil, or loathe the light.
	Peruse this paper. [*Gives him the petition*] 160

Enter LUCIUS[, LEONARDO *and* SILLEUS]

Ferdinand	[*Reads*] Alas, poor man! My soul doth pity him. See, here the villain comes – Lord Lucius, We purpose to prefer you to a wife Of our election.
Lucius	I do beseech your grace to pardon me; I have vow'd to live a single life.
Ferdinand	You have vow'd to live a single villain! Peace, monstrous wretch! I hardly check my tears. Unhappy king that must trust others' ears! No marvel Heaven so many ills down hurl; 170 Naught but injustice can destroy the world. Corrupted judges, the state's most dangerous foes - They smile and strike; there's no 'fence for their blows. Vengeance and rage! I could forget my being And be your executioner myself.
Gisbert	[*aside*] This creature speaks another language.
Silleus	We humbly do confess our crimes and, On our knees, entreat your highness' pardon. [LEONARDO, SILLEUS *and* LUCIUS *kneel*]

Ferdinand	Pardon? May my own sins ne'er be remitted then.
	[*to* LUCIUS] Ingrateful monster! Canst thou deny
	  this schedule? 180
	[*to* GISBERT] Recall thyself, old man; I am thy
	  prince
	And will revenge thy wrong.

Gisbert	Are you a man, sir?
Ferdinand	As thou art.

| | [*to* LUCIUS] Speak, villain. |
| | Canst thou disprove this too just accusation? |

Lucius   I cannot – only for the murder,
            As I shall hope for mercy, I am free.

Gisbert   Lives my Urania, then?

Lucius   I left her near the lodge, whither in grief she made –

Ferdinand   Abhorred viper, that could'st behold her smart
            Who, with her own, cur'd thine, I loathe thy sight   190
            And here deprive thee of all dignity
            Due from thy ancestors. Thy land we seize
            And give thee only four days' space to find Urania
              out.
            One hour deferr'd, our kingly word is past:
            Thou, for her loss, shalt taste untimely death.
            So thrust him forth our presence.
                    [LEONARDO, SILLEUS *and* LUCIUS *rise*]
                    Exeunt [OFFICERS *with*] LUCIUS

Gisbert   [*aside*]   True prince, indeed!
                                          [GISBERT *kneels*]
            [*to* FERDINAND] Pardon, renowned King, my
              much forgetfulness.
            Oh, let some pinnacle, made a god, whose height
            May reach to heaven, bear thy name stamp'd
            In golden characters, untouch'd by envious Time.   200

Ferdinand   Rise, much wrong'd man.   [GISBERT *rises*]
            [*to* LEONARDO *and* SILLEUS] You worst but
              first in place,
            With him that did so easily second thy false doom,

We banish both of you into the woods,
As most unworthy man's society.
[*to* GISBERT] Thou shalt enjoy the place and
　honour
Of our Chief Justice. Infer no denial:
What want is in thy birth's pre-eminence,
Thou hast in virtue and in innocence.
So lead away; thy daughter being not dead,
Thy joy o'erflows, all sorrow's cancelled.　[*Exeunt*]　210

4[.1]

Enter LUCIUS, GULLMAN, FLAVIA, SURDO [*and*] URANIA

Flavia	Perjur'd slave! Hast a wife? Could'st think lechery would have a better end? Out of my doors, seducing varlet!
Lucius	Hear me but speak –
Gullman	Out upon thee, penurious rascal! My flesh shakes to be at thee. Thou hast made little better than a whore of my daughter.
Surdo	And a bawd of your ladyship.
Gullman	Were't not for modesty's sake, I would have my pennyworth's out of thy flesh. 10
Flavia	The hangman will rid us of that care. Beggarly slave! Why dost not laugh at him, Castadora?
Urania	[*aside*] I could shed tears for thee, poor Lucius. Though many months thou couldst endure my grief, One day seems long till I yield thee relief.
Lucius	Is, then, all love and pity banished? In lieu, then, of the good thou stand'st possess'd by me, Grant me but one night's being in thy house.

| | Thou see'st 'tis late, and I unfurnished
Of means and credit. | |
| --- | --- | --- |
| *Flavia* | Would one night save thy life,
Restore thy name and thy degraded honour,
I would not grant it. For know, I hate thee more
Than all thy wealth enforc'd me love before. | 20 |
| *Surdo* | You are no whore? | |
| *Flavia* | So let's in. [*to* LUCIUS] If longer you stay here,
I will provide you of a harbinger. | |
| *Gullman* | You shall have a lodging at the cost of the parish if you stay a little longer.
                        Exeunt [FLAVIA *and* GULLMAN] | |
| *Surdo* | Bawd! Blood-sucker! Cannibal! | |
| *Urania* | Afflicted man,
I, that for comfort sought thy company,
Could now afford some pity unto thee.   *Exit* | 30 |
| *Lucius* | Ill-destined Lucius – but in vain's complaint.
Then, tell me, Surdo, what cure canst thou apply
unto my miseries? | |
Surdo	Such as the world gives to men in distress: as I am a courtier, I must leave you.	
Lucius	How? Leave me?	
Surdo	Would you not have me follow the example of my betters? I promised you to serve you only as you	

	were a lord; and so I have done and will till I see you at the gallows; and thither you shall have followers enough.	40
Lucius	Wilt thou not help to find my wife out, then?	
Surdo	I'll see what I can do. [*Shouts*] Oyez! Did any manner of man take up a woman-child, of the age of twenty-two, lost for want of a husband? Let them look into her mark and if they find her a virgin bring her to the hangman.	
Lucius	Ingrateful groom, dost mock my misery?	
Surdo	Are you such an ass to think she'll be found to save you from hanging that have left her swimming all this while? She has more hope of her widowhood than so. The old saying is: 'Marry a widow whose husband was hanged, and then she cannot upbraid you with them' – I'll see if I can find her and put it in practice. Farewell, I will look to hear from you by the next new ballad. Pray Jove it be to a good tune and come off bravely to the life; 'twill be to your own comfort, and credit of your followers, to see and hear so many bear parts in your death. *Exit*	50 60
Lucius	Contemn'd and left of all! Where are my parasites now? – Honour's shadows, that seem to move with an obsequious right as if they were inseparably tied unto our persons, when the truth is their motion is from the sun which, being down once, we are left naked. Why should I blame this world, then, Since means and honour sway the greatest men? For, give me one that e'er lov'd Virtue poor –	

Show me an usurer charitable or an honest whore!
I cannot, Flavia, with just cause condemn thee;   70
It is the leaden weight of time that moves thy hate
And, with a violent hand, doth force thy soul
To this observing world. For, well thou knowest:
Wert thou as chaste and fair as the Greekish dame
Fam'd for her twice ten winters' constancy,
And hadst no foil to put thy virtues off,
Thou might'st spin out thy days to get thee food,
Or turn base prostitute and sell thy blood
At every comer's price.   [*Lies down on the ground*]

Enter URANIA

Urania   [*apart*] Where might I find this most unhappy man,   80
Whose grief will not permit my jealous soul
To trust him with the night? Oh, did he know
How much beyond myself I prize his love,
'Twould move him to afford me pity, if not love.
But see where, suiting with his fortunes, on the ground
He has cast himself. Could we our fates foreknow,
He had kept the happy mean, not lain so low.
[*to* LUCIUS] My honour'd lord, why with so hard an eye
Do you behold your friends?

Lucius   Thou dost forget thyself. I am poor; and poverty,   90
When none else will do't, makes all men fly.

Urania   You much mistake me, sir. I am Castadora,
One that did never fawn on your prosperity
Yet cannot choose but love you whose sympathy
Speaks mine own woes. Pray, sir, accept this.

Gives him gold

Lucius	O, tell me true:
	Did not Flavia's hand commit this charge to thee?
Urania	Can you yet think she loves you, sir, whose hate
	Has reach'd a height so far above her sex?
	Or is your weakness such to love her still?
Lucius	My constancy is such I ever shall. 100
	Alas, 'tis not her hate but fear to suffer in my
	disgrace – 'tis her want that moves her thus to my
	injury.
Urania	These are the effects of lust, whose seat is in the
	blood
	And sway'd by that as by the nourishing food;
	Whereas love, having her residence only in the soul
	And settling her affections once, is not more mov'd
	By any outward accident than are our thoughts
	By captiving our bodies.
Lucius	Thou speakest beyond a woman. 110
Urania	You have a wife, sir – or, it seems, you had one,
	Though by your much ingratitude undone.
	Compare these two, the strumpet and your wife:
	One seeks your death, the other gives you life.
Lucius	Thy words do trouble me; I am not well.
Urania	Alas, how can you, sir? You are in Hell,
	Tied to the flames of an enchanting harlot.
	Pardon me, sir, if, beyond modesty,
	I press a stranger's ear in whom I see
	My own sad fate. Answer me one demand. 120

Lucius   Freely speak, whate'er it be.

Urania   What one particular
             Most moves your love unto this creature?

Lucius   Her beauty, which alone I would enjoy.

Urania   But never did! What pleasure has the usurer
             In seeing another's gold he cannot hoard?
             Or what particular happiness gives that
             Which, every day, man for a pistolet
             May make purchase on? O, think that, willingly,
             You would not wear the garments of another;
             Nor lay your body in the common bed   130
             Of a suspected harlot. Think how much more
             You should abhor to mix your blood
             With an adulterate courtesan –
             Wash in a lep'rous bath, a strumpet's womb –
             And she your love is such another.

Lucius   Impossible!

Urania   How if I make it apparent?

Lucius   I should die willingly, and think my tortures
             Too gentle for so foul a change.

Urania   Attend me, then.
             Here are three ducats – all the store is left me.
                         [*Puts the money*] *on the ground*
             What will you say if, for this gold, you obtain   140
             To lie with her this night?

Lucius	As I am Lucius, whom she so contemns?
Urania	The same. Embrace her lustful waist, receive As much content as ever; yet, in the morn, She shall reject your sight with loathed scorn.
Lucius	Make me so happy in my misery – My soul shall bless thee.
Urania	An if I do not, may I lose my hopes. Come, saddest soul, your doubts I'll not prolong. [*aside*] Thus honest wives avenge their husband's wrong. *Exeunt* 150

4[.2]

Enter ALEXIS [*and*] ADELIZIA [*at*] *a table* [*bearing food*]

Alexis	How like you, fair, this solitary life?
Adelizia	As shipwreck'd men the shore, or prisoners liberty; I never thought a good in life to be Until I found it here.
Alexis	This, your content, doth bring into my mind Those days that Cavus lived upon his plain – Unhappy courtier, yet a happy swain. Methinks I now do hear his well-tun'd pipe That drew the covetous ear of list'ning shepherds To hear him chant his passed misery – 10

THE POOR MAN'S COMFORT 81

                But I forget myself and stay too long:
                Our supper's yet to kill, and night draws on.

Adelizia   You need not make such haste; our store's not spent.
                Here's enough left; small viands serve content.

Alexis   But time calls forth and promises liberal prey;
                I must be gone. And if my horn you hear,
                Think I have sped. I promise thee rich cheer.

Adelizia   Take your own way.   *Exit* [ALEXIS]
                        Why, now I thank thee, Fate;
                Thou hast made a double 'mends for my lost state.
                Instead of honours and a marriage bed,   20
                To chaste thoughts and content my soul is wed.
                Vain world, I hate thee; 'stead of thy flattery,
                Heaven is my book, virtue my company.

                      Enter OSWELL

Oswell   [*apart*] Where should I seek out death, or find some
                   means
                To stop the gaping jaws of famine?
                I could, on equal terms, encounter with a tiger
                Whose rage hath suck'd her dry. Ingrateful hunger,
                That feeds upon his bowels whose want
                Denies him sustenance, thou wound'st me more
                Than all mine enemies. But see, some angel! –   30
                Yet her face speaks her woman. Meat!
                Should devils guard it, thus would I reach and eat.
                      [OSWELL *approaches the table and eats*]

Adelizia   Amazement to my soul! How greedily he feeds!
                'Twas want, sure, forc'd him hither. If so, I am glad

	our poverty supplies him. Oh, did he know, who, with a liquorish palate, feeds to surfeit, how many empty souls would be made happy in what he vomits – or felt one day's torture of piercing hunger – with what temperate hand he would enjoy these, nature's medicines – food is no other. 40
Oswell	So, I feel myself in reasonable temper now. [*Sees* ADELIZIA] But I forget my happiness – here's a better course. Pardon me, beauty, that I 'scaped so fair a mark as your lips, but now I'll make amends. [*Moves to embrace her*]
Adelizia	What mean you, sir? [*Pushes him away*]
Oswell	Nay, I know you will plead chastity; 'tis the common fault of your sex. You have been some under-vassal, waiting-woman and, fall'n into the butler's hands, had an untimely broaching and now 50 are laid aside here for ripening.
Adelizia	What do you take me for?
Oswell	A woman made for the use of man.
Adelizia	I am a hapless woman, wreck'd at sea And cast upon this shore.
Oswell	Did not I tell you ye had a leak? Come, come, leave circumstance. Thou seest I am mortal, and thou art flesh and blood – born to fall – and therefore let's down together. [OSWELL *takes hold of her.* ADELIZIA *struggles to free herself*]

	THE POOR MAN'S COMFORT	83
	Nay, nay, do not resist.	60
Adelizia	Not resist? Know, brutish creature, I am too well provided to lose mine honour, so long as this frail flesh which we call life can ransom it. [*Draws a knife*] Villain, keep off! Chaste Lucrece shall be my precedent.	
Oswell	So I would have her: lie with Tarquin first and then kill thyself after, if thou hast a mind to't. Lucretia? She was the first cunning whore that ever made a fool of a cuckold. When she saw in the morning her night-villainy was discovered, to prevent the fire, fell upon the sword. But since you'll needs be stabbed, I'll help you. *Takes her knife*	70
Adelizia	Prevented! – If there be a power that helps Distress'd chastity, rescue a spotless maid!	
Oswell	[*aside*] She should be a maid; she's so unwilling to her business. [*to* ADELIZIA] But since you force me to enter into bonds with you, I'll make you seal to the articles of agreement ere I have done with you. [*Ties her up*]	
Adelizia	Help, help! If I have deserv'd thine anger, Heaven, Oh, let it fall at once! Let one death expiate. [*Lets fall*] *a letter*	80
Oswell	[*aside*] She should be a sinner; death's so often in her mouth. What's here? [OSWELL *picks up the letter*] Epistles? [*Reads*] 'To the high and mighty Prince Ferdinand –' From whence? 'Yours, Valerio of Sicily'. 'We have sent you here our daughter' –	

	Fortune, thou hast return'd amends for all my wrongs. Revenge, I will not keep thee fasting one minute longer. *Horn within*	
Adelizia	Heaven, thou art just! Now, monster, do thy worst!	90
Oswell	Beyond Hell's torture! What villain blows that horn?	
Adelizia	A virtuous woodman who, with his followers –	
Oswell	His followers? Nay, then, I am trapp'd; the bellowing ox, that with his groans did fright the earth, carried not half that torture in't. I shall dissolve through fear –	
Adelizia	– the baseness of thy guilt, unworthy wretch! Yet, know how worthy merit stands: I pity thee. Distract thyself no further. By my chaste blood, I'll set thee free, so henceforth to this wood thou wilt become a stranger.	100
Oswell	Hell swallow me, else.	
Adelizia	I'll take your oath. Unbind me first, then fall to your meat with as good stomach as before. [OSWELL *unties her*]	

Enter ALEXIS, LEONARDO [*and*] SILLEUS

| *Alexis* | Recall your spirits, grief-afflicted men.
Time may restore those honours he hath borrowed –
'Tis but to try how you will bear it.
Nor shall I think it my least happiness
To have been author of your change. |

Both	Your virtuous arguments have overcome us.	110
Alexis	Now, lady, I have brought you – Ha! What stranger's that?	
Adelizia	A miserable, almost famish'd man; He hardly could speak well when he came in: His body was so weak, his mind so ill.	
Oswell	[*aside*] She'll spoil all. [*to* ALEXIS] I was a poor soldier in these wars and have been in some reputation with our King. I have been troublesome to this gentlewoman. I would fain be unmannerly: having filled my belly, be out of this forest.	120
Adelizia	His guilt admits no trust. Pray, give him free conduct.	
Alexis	[*to* OSWELL] I'll force your stay. Since we have met thus happily, We will not part till supper; no place I see But gives us means to practise charity. What wants in fare, your welcome shall supply. – Make good my promise, lady.	
Adelizia	With a willing heart. [*aside*] If you knew all, you'd say I had reason for't. *Exeunt* [ADELIZIA *and* ALEXIS]	
Oswell	[*aside*] Hell choke you with your supper! But may these two be Silleus and Leonardo that help'd to disthrone me? What new turn of state has forc'd them hither?	130

Leonardo	[*to* SILLEUS] I'll question him; it may be he can resolve us if Oswell lives. [*to* OSWELL] Methought I heard thee name thy dependence on the banish'd King?
Oswell	I did hang on him, as others did, as long as he had nap – you ha' my meaning. Came you not from court?
Silleus	Against our wills. For know, we are banish'd thence by unmindful Ferdinand who, for one bad, has quite 140 forgot the many goods he still enjoys by us.
Oswell	I know't too well. [*aside*] Hell take you for't!
Leonardo	Leaving our merits, let it suffice He turn'd us down that by our aid did rise. Can you resolve, sir, if Oswell live?
Oswell	And if I could, think'st I would betray him? I'd suffer first –
Leonardo	Protest no further; There's none here means him less good than yourself.
Oswell	[*aside*] This falls out to my wish. [*to* LEONARDO *and* SILLEUS] A word with you, gentlemen. Suppose Oswell lived and, by your aid, 150 might repossess his diadem. Would you prove honest?
Both	As Heaven to virtue!

Oswell	Then know, I am the man and to regain my crown want only your assistance.
Both	Command us as your vassals.
Oswell	– as our friends, and those that shall have equal shares with us. First, then, know this woman is Valerius' daughter.
Leonardo	The woman of this cave? 160
Oswell	The same, sent hither to be match'd with Sigismond and, shipwreck'd in her passage, fell upon this shore.
Both	A most strange accident!
Oswell	'Tis her disgrace or death must raise our hopes.
Leonardo	How is this to be made possible?
Oswell	Thus: myself, not taking notice of her birth, will charge her to the state for companying in lustful action with this woodman; which, seconded by you, will seem so clear that, being returned with 170 shame or here with death paying her forfeiture, her father, that overwhelm'd our state, in just revenge bears us up again.
Both	A most unheard-of villainy!
Oswell	Do you demur upon't?
Both	We only want disguise – that, and 'tis done.

Oswell	Here's gold to furnish you. [*Gives them money*] This night I'll raise the neighbouring village to apprehend 'em. Make you hence and fail not tomorrow to meet me in the Senate. 180
Leonardo	Our lives be gag'd; if we one minute miss, Be this the last day of our happiness. *Exeunt* [LEONARDO *and* SILLEUS]
Oswell	Your wishes be your own. - Thou Queen of Fate, Forbear thy restless motion but one hour, Revenge is mine; Oswell's above thy power! *Exit*

5[.1]

Enter LUCIUS and URANIA

Urania	Have I not kept my promise? Did you not find her base and mercenary?
Lucius	She is, as all the world is, mercenary – Except thyself, chaste, virtuous Castadora.

Enter GULLMAN [and] FLAVIA

Gullman	[*apart*] But art sure he has no more gold?
Flavia	Not an asper, but I'll try. [*to* LUCIUS] Come, you dissembling wanton, thou dost not know how I love thee! Hast ne'er a toy, a ring nor jewel left?
Lucius	Pardon, sweet Flavia, I ha' not any. Yet such is thy impulsive and attracting beauty, I can as well live without free air as be debarred thy presence.
Flavia	How's this? My presence?
Gullman	The fellow's desperate – he would fain be hang'd at our door. We want no sign: good wine needs no bush. We have custom enough already.
Lucius	[*to* FLAVIA] Thou dost but put this trick on me to try me. Thy last night's love show'd thy affection to me.

10

Flavia	Affection? Marry, faugh! I would not endure such another night's torment. Pack hence, or call an officer.	20
Lucius	Thy worst, foul monster; I will not leave this place. Was't thou as high in malice as in lust, Here will I end my life to prove Heaven just.	
Urania	[*to* FLAVIA] Let me entreat you: for this day, forbear him.	
Gullman	Out upon thee, puritanical filth! We may thank thee for this that prefer'st the cart before the horse – turn'st procurer before th'art past procreation.	
Flavia	This young bawd will confound all our doings. [*to* URANIA] I shall set you in with a mischief.	30
Urania	Thou hast done thy worst already, and my miseries, In spite of thee, shall end. [*aside*] This hour doth gain My Lucius' love, or kills me with disdain. [*Exit*]	
Gullman	[*to* LUCIUS] You will not go, then?	
Lucius	Not stir from hence.	
Gullman	Look to the door, daughter, while I go for the constable. [*to* LUCIUS] Wouldst make a vaulting-school of our house? Thou may'st hang thyself an thou wilt but not here, neither. Yet if thou hast a mind to't, I'll go fetch a hangman. *Exit*	

THE POOR MAN'S COMFORT

Flavia She tells you true. This, in a circle, follows: 40
Fools and knaves nourish us, and we the gallows.
Exit

Lucius Monsters in nature! My apprehensive thoughts
Present a thousand tortures, the least of which
Wounds more than the bloodiest executioner.
Thou tell-tale Conscience, cease thy bawling
   clamours;   [*Draws a dagger*]
Here's that shall stop thy throat. Yet now I think on't
My poor Urania died a ling'ring death,
Each thought whereof, like to a greedy vulture,
Feeds on my tired heart.

Enter URANIA

                     Thou discontented ghost,
Where'er thou wand'rest, stay thy restless course. 50
Behold thy most ingrateful husband's blood
Sating the thirsty earth; and thus, Urania,
I boldly come to thee –

[LUCIUS *prepares to stab himself.* URANIA *stays his arm*]

Urania And thou art welcome as heaven to misery.
Mistake me not: I am Urania –
She that in this shape pursued thy wished sight,
Attending this bless'd hour.

Lucius   Urania?
Shame and my joys at once confound me.
Canst thou forgive my wrongs?

Urania	As freely As I wish forgiveness of my sins. Say but thou lovest me, I have double Interest for my sorrow.	60
Lucius	Love thee? I am thy vassal; my joys come on so fast, I fear they are too violent to last. [*Embraces her*]	

Enter FLAVIA

Flavia	[*apart*] I think here comes a surserare to remove you. How's this? Lucius and my maid so familiar? [*to* URANIA] Impudent strumpet! I'll tear the flesh off thy face! [*Rushes to strike* URANIA]	
Lucius	Perpetual hag, take this for't! [*Stabs her*]	
Flavia	Devils and furies! I am slain! [*Dies*]	70
Urania	Alas, what hast thou done?	
Lucius	Nothing but what my life must answer. Fly, my Urania! Though thou forgav'st me, Heaven will not; By what thou hold'st most dear, abandon me.	
Urania	No, should the racks and tortures presently Be fix'd unto my limbs.	
Lucius	Thou add'st to my afflictions. If prayers will not prevail, I'll fly and leave thee.	
Urania	Rather of life than of thy sight bereave me.	

	Know, I will accuse myself as chiefest actor in this murder, if thou makest motion to go without me.	80

Enter GULLMAN, CONSTABLE *and* OFFICER

Gullman	See, this is the flesh-fly I told you of! Open that box; you may swear lawfully you took no bribe of me. Constable, do your office. [*Sees* FLAVIA] Oh, my daughter! Constable, my daughter!	
Constable	How came this murder?	
Lucius	This bloody hand did do it.	
Urania	— set on by me!	
Gullman	Let me tear her eyes out! [OFFICER *restrains* GULLMAN]	
Lucius	By all that may be sworn by, she is free; The act is only mine.	
Gullman	Most unnatural villain to thrust a woman into the body thus unmanly. I will have both your bloods for't.	90
Urania	Mine; he is innocent.	
Lucius	Mine; I desire it.	
Gullman	Nay, ne'er strive. I'll hang you both, I warrant you. My daughter was not unknown to some of the bench, and if they would not speak for her in such a case as this, would they might never have good of	

woman's flesh. Oh, my daughter! My chaste and
virtuous daughter! *Exeunt* 100

5[.2]

Enter SIGISMOND *and* CATZO [*dressed*] *as a lady*

Sigismond	Thou art a lady, fair one.
Catzo	Ay, a horrible, painted one.
Sigismond	And a mighty great one, and therefore I'll court thee. [*Approaches* CATZO *with amorous intent*]
Catzo	'Tis beyond the art of man to court me fair. I am not to be dealt withal in that kind, and therefore keep off! I am not for your turn. Keep off, saucy jack!
Sigismond	Not for my turn? Why, I am a prince, and will engirt thy brow, thy ivory brow, with stones as precious. 10
Catzo	Stones? You can do no good upon me with your stones.
Sigismond	Grant me but assurance of thy love, I'll dart against Jove's thunder – my rival Jove, whose bolt did cleave my heart through and through, and made a broad way to my brain when I last courted thee in yonder thicket.
Catzo	[*aside*] Oh horrible! He has got the true property of a lover: he can lie bravely. [*to* SIGISMOND] Court me in yonder thicket? 20

Sigismond	Why? Hast thou forgot, my sweet duck? Look on me, my pigsny. Cast but one smile, one gentle smile, upon me.
Catzo	[*aside*] Some smile? I cannot smile for laughing!
Sigismond	Well, remember this. You will not afford me a sheep's eye? Say no more – nay, ne'er entreat. Thou get'st not a kiss, a look, nor a touch, nor a feel, nor a bit of my thumb's length.
Catzo	[*aside*] That's but short allowance for a gentlewoman. 30
Sigismond	[*aside*] I must to her again. [*to* CATZO] You do not love me; you do not. Alas, I am ignorant of your tricks. You have forgot since you and I played last at maw, when your ace of hearts could not command my knave of diamonds till you were glad to lay your five fingers on't.
Catzo	Maw? [*aside*] Fie upon him, what a noddy is this?
Sigismond	You have forgot since I talk'd bawdy with your ladyship by moonshine; and how you swore you dream'd of me till you tickled again, and ever since 40 doted on me with the very conceit of the dream; and now I will make your ladyship kneel for a kiss. Nay, humble thyself, and I will not come over thee.
Catzo	[*aside*] Fie, fie, never had gentlewoman such a suitor! Now, by my poting-stick (a fit oath for a

	chambermaid!), you shall have him court me in all the true elements of a drunkard: fox-like, lion-like and last, maudlin-like; and so turn all his smiles into tears.	50
Sigismond	[*aside*] Not yet? Will she not stoop? I must close with her. [*to* CATZO] Come, come, I know you swell now – you grow so plump about the lips. Suppose I should vouchsafe to kiss this chop-cherry, now?	
Catzo	I scorn to kiss, I can assure thee.	
Sigismond	Disdain a prince, a lion? Cur, trash, parboil'd stuff! What's woman but a hollow vessel, an aqua-vitae bottle, a washing-tub, a box? What is your ladyship proud of?	60
Catzo	Of my virginity, sir.	
Sigismond	I'll try what kind of stuff your ladyship's virginity's made of. [SIGISMOND *takes hold of* CATZO]	
Catzo	Thou wilt not ravish me, wilt thou?	
Sigismond	By Mars' standard, but I will.	
Catzo	By Venus' buckler, but thou shalt not. [*Puts a hand to his sword*]	
Sigismond	Thou wilt not draw, I hope?	
Catzo	But I will, and defend my maiden honour with my life. [*Brandishes the sword at* SIGISMOND]	

Sigismond	Put up, fair maid; thy chastity o'ercomes my spleen. Forgive me, gentle love, and I will weep myself to water.	70
Catzo	[*aside*] That may be, for your brain swims, I am sure. What an ass is this to be in love with me? [*to* SIGISMOND] I am no lady, sir; I am your man, Catzo.	
Sigismond	Keep off! I shall o'erwhelm thee else. [*Moves as if on the sea*] Dost not see me swim and tumble mountain-high? Thou art a pinnace, art thou?	
Catzo	A kind of a fly-boat. [*Moves up and down*] There's a storm toward; my best is to put into harbour.	80
Sigismond	Sea-room enough, or we are lost! Amain, amain! Now up, now down again! *Tumbles about*	
Catzo	I am sure I have a leak already. Help, help, help!	

Enter FERDINAND[, LICURGO *and* GLISCO]

Ferdinand	What means this outcry?	
Catzo	I think he has thrust out my bottom. I shall never live to prove the old proverb true – a young courtier and an old beggar – I have had so many maims in his service.	
Sigismond	Neptune has laid the storm. How calm's the sea now! How silent the winds! All's done, all's done.	90
Catzo	All's one for that; you shall not draw me to sea with you again.	

Ferdinand	[*to* CATZO] How camest thou thus attired?
Catzo	He said he would make a lady on me but, as many knights do, he has made a poor one of me. He began very hotly but at last he cool'd me over head and ears. He handle a lady?
Ferdinand	This makes me think that love was the original of this untimely ecstasy. Didst never hear him speak of some strange beauty?
Catzo	He spoke too lately with me; and now I remember me, I left him in the wood with a good handsome female, and when I found him again he was as mad as a hart in rutting-time.

Enter VINCENTIO

Ferdinand	Her sight, sure, did transport him. What news, Vincentio?
Vincentio	No great news: only a woodman and a maid, accus'd of foul lust, this day receive their doom.
Ferdinand	Where were they taken?
Vincentio	In an obscure cave within the forest.
Sigismond	That maid would I fain deal withal. [*to* VINCENTIO] Command her hither. Why dost not fetch her?

Ferdinand	Be patient; thou shalt along with us. Dost know the face that late, i'th'forest, lost you?
Catzo	I have cause to know it. They talk of countenances – I got more by that face in an hour than the best countenance i'th'court will get me in an age, though I were usher to the best lady of them all.
Ferdinand	[*aside*] My heart presages good; Heaven, work thy will. When we least hope, the heavens prove kindest still. 120 [*to* CATZO] Sirrah, bring him along. *Exit*
Catzo	Come, sir, will you jog into the garden?
Sigismond	You'll bring me to the lady, then?
Catzo	Yes, presently; as soon as ever we can overtake her. *Exeunt*

5[.3]

Enter GISBERT as a senator, [VINCENTIO] with others, OSWELL, ALEXIS, ADELIZIA [and] OFFICERS. [Barrier or railing to suggest] a bar [and seats to represent] a Senate.

Gisbert	Stand forth, Alexis. [ALEXIS *stands at the bar*] Though my soul doth tell me Thy thoughts are clear from foul unchastity, Yet since thy accuser, by just course of law,

| | Pursues thy life, thou must endure the hand |
| | Of peerless justice. |

Alexis   I crave no other.
          Let equal combat prove us worthy death,
          Or else just vengeance stop his perjur'd breath.

Oswell   I seal to thy request if, in one hour, two witnesses
          besides myself do not make good this accusation.

Gisbert   Your offer stands confirm'd. Officer-at-Arms,   10
          If, ere the appointed time, these witnesses
          Make no appearance, bring into the lists
          Those combatants equally prepar'd.

Officer   It shall be done.

Gisbert   Although my place forbids to do thee other right,
          Alexis, yet this comfort I will give thee which
          stands for all:
          No power were just, if guiltless men should fall.

Alexis   I have no other hope; who bears a spotless breast
          Doth want no comfort else, howe'er distress'd.   20

Adelizia That speaks our happiness for, spite of destiny,
          We can nor live nor die unhappily.
          [*aside*] However, I'll conceal my parentage.
                Exeunt [OFFICER, OSWELL, ADELIZIA
                                    and ALEXIS]

Gisbert   What other cause depends to crave our hearing?

          Enter CONSTABLE, GULLMAN, LUCIUS,
                URANIA [*and* OFFICER]

Constable	Bring 'em forth! Away with 'em! [OFFICER *brings* LUCIUS *and* URANIA *to the bar*]
Vincentio	How now, what noise is this?
Gullman	Justice, let me have justice, noble senators!
Gisbert	Speak freely, woman; thou shalt have thy wish.
Gullman	Behold the bloody murderers of my innocent daughter! 30
Gisbert	How? Lucius one of 'em? Vile wretch, Dost thou not know this day doth end thy life If thou shalt fail to find thy hapless wife?
Lucius	That sentence thus is void: I here present Your daughter and my wife. [LUCIUS *and* URANIA *approach* GISBERT]
Gisbert	My daughter!
Urania	Oh, think that I am lost still, or that you ne'er Were happy in the enjoyment of a child. For know, I stand guilty of this abhorred murder.
Lucius	She wrongs her innocent soul; 'twas this hand did it In just mov'd anger.
Urania	But 'twas I that bid him, 40 And that in law is principal.

Gullman   Between 'em both I have lost my daughter – a very
         chaste virgin and a virtuous.

Lucius   A noted whore, a courtesan!

Gisbert   Divided soul, in what amazement stand'st thou?
         On this hand Justice stands, but here a father.
         Nature, thou art powerful in me; immaculate robes,
         You shall not blush at my partiality.
                                     [*Rises from his seat*]

Vincentio What mean you, sir?

Gisbert   To be a man, a father: oh, my Urania!   50

Vincentio This violent passion needs not, sir. Possess
         Your seat again.

Gisbert   It suits not with my fortunes.
         [*to* SENATORS] Vouchsafe me leave to plead her
           cause, you worthy judges.
         Behold three lives laid in a doubtful scale,
         'Gainst which a strumpet's lust the balance sways.
         Three worthy lives – if age and fate deny
         To make mine miserable – which, if your gentler
           hands
         Refuse to poise, are lost and must pay the price
         Of an adulteress' blood. Oh, think what a whore is!
         A creature only shap'd like woman that we might see 60
         In that fair foil best her deformity;
         The womb of sin, from whence all horrid crimes
         As rivulets from the sea derive their streams;
         The Devil's warehouse, for though we 'void all
           snares

	This surely takes, and here he vends his wares
	Which no shop else would utter; hence avarice,
	Pride, pale murder, all black deeds do rise. Besides,
	Think how she stands in law to whom's denied
	A Christian burial – this law by which we are tried.
	Oh, let it not exact such payment, then: 70
	For those deserve not common rights of men.
	This is the only favour I do crave:
	Judge her unworthy life as of a grave.
Vincentio	Your arguments are forcible; only let's know
	The motives to her death.
Lucius	Her sensual rage brought her into the place
	Where, much unlook'd for, joy forc'd one embrace.
	The wretch at sight whereof, o'ercome with spleen
	Or hateful jealousy, with violent hands
	Did seize my wife; which sight on sudden rais'd 80
	My just incensed blood that, with one stroke,
	Her cursed life unhappily I took.
Gisbert	[*to* SENATORS] Make it your own case: think how free they stood,
	In height of their own joys, from other's blood.
Vincentio	The case is plain: she sought her own death wilfully
	And, seeking her own ill, we judge them free.
	[*to* GISBERT] Now take your place again.
Gisbert	Bear witness, I have play'd a father's part.
Vincentio	A careful father.

Lucius and Urania	One most kind and loving.
Gisbert	Let me embrace you both. [*Embraces them*] Farewell. 90 Think here your father dies, and now y'are To be doom'd by an impartial judge.
Vincentio	What means this circumstance?
Gisbert	Know that a man consists of soul and body; The one by Nature, the other by Justice rul'd. So, he is less than man that swerves from either And disobeys these equal governors. What Nature might command I have perform'd. Now, Justice takes his place, true partless Justice – That heavenly name's bestow'd upon us here 100 That we, like gods, might no affection bear; Which once again commands unto the bar Those bloody murderers.

[OFFICER *leads* LUCIUS *and* URANIA *to the bar.*
GISBERT *resumes his seat*]

Vincentio	Strange and unheard of.
Gisbert	Stand forth, you hapless wretches, that have robb'd A creature of her life, which to restore Would make the world turn bankrupt. Nay, more, You have robb'd Heaven of a soul, enforc'd her hence Loaden with all her sins without defence; Not given her time to shed one penitent tear 110 That might plead for her before that severe And all-confounding Judge. With loss of breath,

| | You have repriev'd her soul to far worse death.
Lastly, you have feloniously usurp'd
The sword of government, violated law
And, being born subjects, you have assum'd
The seat of death-inflicting sovereignty;
For which we doom you –
Weak heart, why dost thou faint? Thou injurest me.
You traitorous eyes, since that you dare not see
To do such worthy justice on these wretches,
I will blind and bar that light
Whose partial view do make so few do right.
Now know, we doom you, for this your horrid murder,
To present execution, and command
That where the fact was done a gibbet stand
On which you both shall suffer forthwith.- Officers away;
Your lives are forfeit in one hour's delay. | 120 |
| --- | --- | --- |
| *Vincentio* | Beyond all precedent! | |
| *Lucius* | [*to* GISBERT]   For mine own life,
'Tis justly forfeited; but to this creature,
Urania, not as she is my wife
But thy daughter, the hope of thy name
And wish'd posterity, be pitiful. | 130 |
| *Gisbert* | Thou beat'st the air. Though all the world should fail,
Justice must be herself – bear equal sail. | |
| *Urania* | [*to* LUCIUS] Be patient, gentle love; since 'tis for thee
I cannot think it is an ill to die. | |

	[*to* GISBERT] Father, farewell; your doom I will not grudge.	
	Above I hope to find a milder judge.	
Gisbert	Away with 'em. Heaven on their souls have mercy.	140
	[OFFICERS *take hold of* LUCIUS *and* URANIA]	

Enter FERDINAND

Ferdinand	Stay, let me embrace thee, thou perfect'st man	
	That e'er made Nature proud. Renowned Gisbert,	
	Lo, as thou gavest unto thy country's good	
	Thy only daughter, having no other gift	
	Worthy thy merit, I return again	
	Thy present, which to recompense	
	With any other benefit would speak us poor	
	And much ingrateful; in us they both	
	Shall live with pardon. So, receive them, then –	
Gisbert	As a reprieve sent to condemned men!	150
	[*Embraces them*]	
Ferdinand	– in whom may'st thou survive to endless days.	
	As for this loathed creature [*indicating* GULLMAN],	
	Hell's harbinger, this bawd to Sin, her daughter's	
	loss shall take away her body's punishment; only, we	
	banish her six miles from any city.	
Gullman	I had rather be carted six times about the city than live in the country, unless your grace will make a continual progress.	
Ferdinand	Away with her!	
	Exeunt [OFFICER *with* GULLMAN]	

                              [*Tucket*]
                    What means this sound?

Vincentio   It gives a signal to a combatant that has accus'd a   160
               stranger of foul lust with a known shepherd.

Ferdinand   Ourself have heard so much.

               Enter [OFFICER *with*] OSWELL [*in arms and
               disguised*], ALEXIS [*in arms, and*] ADELIZIA.
               SIGISMOND *gazes on her.*

                                    Give him his oath.

Vincentio   [*to* OSWELL] Swear, by thy trust in Heaven, thou
                 com'st not arm'd
               Led on by malice or in hope of gain,
               But in the justice of thy cause, without
               Either charm or guile.

Oswell   This I'll make good.

Ferdinand   Administer the like oath to the other.

Vincentio   [*to* ALEXIS] Swear by the equal powers, no hope or
                 confidence
               Doth raise thine arm, besides thine innocence.

Alexis   I swear, and if not truly, of Heaven I crave,   170
               Instead of aid, to send a shameful grave.

Ferdinand   Give signal to the fight.

Sigismond   Stay!

Ferdinand	What means our son?
Sigismond	'Tis she! That brow, that eye, that face doth speak it. Give me my armour there.
Catzo	[*aside*] Give him his brains there – h'as most need of them.
Sigismond	[*to* CATZO] Villain, I'll tear thy soul out if thou defer one minute! [*to* ADELIZIA] Divinest beauty – oh, let me kiss thy hand!
Ferdinand	This accident confounds me. Speak, gentle son.
Sigismond	[*to* FERDINAND] And if I have a being worthy you 180 Deny not my request, or with my breast I'll naked, thus, oppose the traitor.
Ferdinand	Thou hast thy wish, fair son. [*to* OFFICER] Bring weapons forth. [*aside*] Some fate directs him thus. [*Exit* OFFICER]

Enter LEONARDO [*and*] SILLEUS [*both in arms and disguised*]

Vincentio	More champions yet? What mean these strangers?
Leonardo	To prove this traitor a malicious villain, That lady chaste and free.
Silleus	The same cause moveth me to equal arms.

Sigismond	You shall be damn'd first! By my blood and honour, Who makes an offer to deprive this arm Of this fair conquest draws one on himself.	190
Ferdinand	They shall not; [*to* LEONARDO *and* SILLEUS] I must entreat you Give free way unto his passion, Being assur'd the hand of Heaven Draws him to end his life or misery.	
Leonardo and Silleus	Shall we not have the honour, then?	
Ferdinand	Our son has begg'd it and it must be his.	
Both	We'll free him from that danger. *Discover themselves*	
Oswell	[*aside*] Vexation!	
Ferdinand	How dare you, being exil'd, approach this place?	
Leonardo	Though not from death, this deed shall free one stain. Know that our love to justice, whose wrong erst lost our good names, doth force us hither. This is traitorous Oswell! [*Pulls off* OSWELL's *disguise*]	200
Ferdinand	Oswell? Lay hands upon the monster! [OFFICERS *seize him*]	
Silleus	[*Indicating* ADELIZIA] This, Adelizia, King Valerius' daughter,	

	To whose untimely fall that villain brib'd us;	
	When this bless'd shepherd, that preserv'd her breath,	
	Redeem'd our lives from a despised death.	
Ferdinand	Astonishment!	
Alexis	Dread sovereign, accept this beauteous princess, fair Adelizia, by me preserv'd after her shipwreck.	210
	[*Presents her to* FERDINAND *with a letter*]	
Ferdinand	Joy overcomes me. Can Adelizia live?	
Adelizia	That letter speaks no less.	
Sigismond	[*to* ADELIZIA] I know you are the same my love pursued	
	In those spacious woods.	
Adelizia	I am the same.	
Ferdinand	Thou hast reviv'd my son, restor'd mine age!	
	So many blessings, heaven – I wish no more.	
Adelizia	If any good my being brings with it,	
	This virtuous shepherd well may challenge it.	
Ferdinand	Our love and high regard shall speak it freely.	220
	[*to* LEONARDO *and* SILLEUS] To you we give your means and liberty.	
	[*to* OSWELL] To thee –	
Leonardo and Silleus	Do but command us! We'll tear him piecemeal.	

Ferdinand	Though his desert to such extremes might sway, We'll have no blood shed on our wedding-day. We doom him to perpetual 'prisonment –
Oswell	Had I my will, You should all keep your wedding-day in hell!

Ferdinand	So, lead him hence.
	         [*Exeunt* OSWELL *and* OFFICERS]
	           Now, fair Adelizia, there remains
	 Only thy free consent to accept my son.

Sigismond	I am her own – the marriage heaven begun 230 When her bless'd sight restor'd me.
Ferdinand	Speak, gentle maid.
Adelizia	Since Fate ordains it so, I like your son so well I'll scarce say no.
Ferdinand	Then, lovely daughter, true subjects, worthy friends, I embrace you all, and here our woes all end; Which teacheth us, howe'er vain man may trust, The end makes happy those only that are just.

FINIS

Glossarial Notes

Prologue

5	*ingrate*	ungrateful
6	*adulterate*	adulterous
8	*like*	please
11	*Per E. M.*	indicating that the prologue was written by E. M., perhaps Edward May, an actor, who is also mentioned in the copy of *Edmund Ironside* included with *Poor Man* in the Egerton MS.

1[.1]

1	*only beauty*	beauty alone
2	*force kings leave*	the text omits 'to' before a verb here and at ll 4 and 17
5	*new-fall'n*	newborn
18	*roundelays*	short songs associated with pastoral singing contests
20	*firstlings*	first offspring of an animal
29	*does charge*	is impetuous, makes a violent assault
32	*forbear*	cease
44	*approve*	corroborate or confirm
61	*time-observing fox*	renowned for waiting for its opportunity
73	*Beshrew*	to wish evil on
77	*styles*	phrases, perhaps verses
84	*affect*	love
86	*gage*	pledge, security
104	*possess thee of*	give thee
106	*this uncertain good*	all worldly fortune
109	*beadsman*	person paid to pray for another's soul
111	*afford*	give
119	*work*	not only persuade, but have sex with
121	*turn tail*	run away, but also lose an erection

125	*soundly*	well, healthily
129	*scurvily*	despicably, with pun on scurvy, the disease
132	*smart*	pain
156	*chincough*	whooping cough
157	*usurer's disease*	perhaps possession of a tapeworm – to explain the usurer's greed
159	*feeling's gone*	loss of sexual arousal
174	*dance where*	have sexual intercourse with
175	*shake my heels*	dance, again with sexual innuendo

1[.2]

3	*virginal jacks*	keys of the virginal, a small piano-like instrument
6	*making with*	making alliance with
12	*bootless*	pointless
27	*want*	lack
28	*experient*	experienced
54	*melancholy*	thought to derive from an excess of black choler in the body, causing fear and sorrow in the sufferer
60	*cabinet*	case for safe-keeping of jewels or other valuables
63-4	*Beyond this ... dare thy fate*	you might dare Fate to exceed this cross
67	*recognizance*	token or emblem
71	*crooked piece*	physically/morally deviant person
78	*want*	lack
88	*tears*	one of the hyena's human tricks
91	*not off*	not catch light
97	*tabor*	small drum
105	*counterfeit*	portrait
107	*run a tilt*	engage in a tilt or joust, either against an opponent or aiming at a stationary target. Also term for sexual intercourse
107	*nose*	the target, with phallic undertones
108	*fathoms*	one fathom equivalent to the length of a man's forearm

108	*in his light*	in his perspective
109-10	*takes it in snuff*	takes offence
110	*rails*	complains bitterly
111	*pare*	cut
112	*collops*	slices of meat
116	*boot*	advantage
116	*stay by it*	remain and listen
121	*crown*	of his head, as opposed to the royal crown
127-8	*here be they*	referring to the coins
135	*ingrateful*	unfriendly, harsh

1[.3]

2	*Hymen*	Greek and Roman god of marriage
12	*post*	messenger
12	*scouring*	ranging in search of something
16	*published*	proclaimed in public
21	*erst*	formerly
49	*distemper'd*	vexed, put in a bad humour
50	*pale*	pallor
53	*give colour*	countenance or excuse, also to blush
72	*abjure*	renounce, abstain from
78	*chapman*	agent or broker
84	*untruss*	undress, communal part of wedding celebrations
84	*lubber*	big, stupid fellow but also sailor's term for a clumsy seaman. Putting to sea was a metaphor for sexual consummation
85	*he must to hose go down*	hose were stockings or breeches – sailors wore a particular wide-legged version
90	*get*	beget
90	*chopping*	strapping
92	*standing-table*	symbol of permanent hospitality
93-4	*free stock …open house*	with implication of sexual infidelity
97	*crowns*	coins

102	*forbearance*	abstention, delay
108	*thrifty*	flourishing, thriving
109	*commits sin with himself*	enjoys a private pleasure, with onanistic undertone
113	*court midwife*	one who would attend many secret, illegitimate births
116	*he's sold all*	seventeenth-century English aristocrats were famously reduced to financial hardship and forced to sell their lands
127-8	*Art and Nature…make perfect*	Art and Nature were often coupled together in discussions of beauty. In the case of women, Art usually represents cosmetics
132	*gull*	fool or cheat
136	*Arcadia*	part of Greece, famous idealised setting of pastoral literature
156	*music*	barking of the hounds
161	*thou Roman captive*	most likely the story of a runaway slave, Androcles, who extracted the thorn from a lion's paw and was later recognised and spared by the lion when they met in the arena
163	*reasonless*	incapable of reason, also without cause
186	*younglings*	young animals
195	*questionable*	in doubt

2[.1]

2	*soil*	country
2	*airy*	heavenly
8	*unhallowed*	not consecrated as site for burial
14	*casements*	eyelids
15	*Morpheus*	Greek god of sleep and dreams
17	*ill-starr'd*	ill-destined
19	*Want best discovers idol Majesty*	deprivation reveals true royalty, with a pun on 'idle', untested
20	*Ho! Illo, illo, illo!*	hunting cry

GLOSSARIAL NOTES

22	*gelder*	one who gelds or castrates animals
22	*getting*	begetting
23	*horn*	hunting-horn and synonym for phallus
25	*tame you*	by giving him a venereal disease
31	*unfeed*	unpaid
33-4	*lies as her mother taught her*	on her back
36-7	*ride her*	mount in sexual sense
40-2	*turns up ... punk or a Puritan*	to show the whites of the eyes could be taken as an expression of affected devotion, associated here with prostitutes who pretend to be virgins and Puritans who fake piety
53-4	*precious stone*	virginity was often described as a jewel
57	*yet but for one*	yet for only one
64-5	*may take my payment otherwise*	by robbing the bodies
69	*executor*	by bestowing their property on himself
73	*moves this stay*	motivates this delay
84-5	*breath ... second soul*	according to Genesis, God breathed soul into man
93	*speechless ecstasy*	silent stupor
95	*insensual*	lewd, unchaste
96	*I would, should all*	I would do this if all
139	*thunderbolt*	Jove was famous for using these as weapons
141-2	*Europa ... bull's back*	in Greek mythology, Jove abducted the princess Europa by transforming into a bull and carrying her across the sea on his back
142-3	*My kingdom for a boat*	allusion to Shakespeare's *Richard III* where the king cries 'My kingdom for a horse', 5.7.7.
143	*mussel boat*	OED suggests a mussel shell used as a toy boat by children
145	*Souse*	not clear, probably a reference to the sea in which he will 'souse' or plunge himself

2[.2]

10-11	*True stitch ... past that shortly*	Gullman takes 'stitch' in the

	sense of a sudden pain, with the implication that Urania will soon get over her first painful experience of sex
13	*laid her hand ...good pieces* a running joke on the association of needle with penis, and of needlework with prostitution Compare with the Hostess in *Henry V*, 2.1.33-6
16	*a pair of hangers* pieces of decorative tapestry, but also perhaps illegitimate offspring
31	*jacks* knaves, poorer clients
32	*rise* literally by being lifted onto horse, also through financial and social status of client
33	*comes a-horseback* sign of social status, but also to climax whilst 'riding' woman
39	*painted staff* staff of office, only superficially virtuous
41	*come off at her pleasure* experience sexual climax
42	*keep her mill a-going* satisfy her sexually
43	*turn him off* pass him over, push him off after sex
57-8	*heavy night on't ... burden,* referring to women bearing the weight of men in sex
67	*backside* back yard
67	*stirring will get you a stomach* exercise will give you appetite
75	*in the suds* in difficulties or disgrace, pregnant
76	*Time shall be false to truth first* play on the proverbial maxim 'Truth is the daughter of Time'
79	*so ta'en off* i.e. kissed away
96	*arrantest* most utter
97	*tiring* feeding greedily
97	*ringtail* female harrier-hen
106	*mend it* alter or repent it
114	*been with* visited/slept with
114	*conjurer* associated with the supernatural, created visions
124-5	*French thing* the French crown, also perhaps syphilis
125	*you wot on* you know of
132	*maidenhead* their first airing
132	*for* going to see

133	*the show*	presumably the investiture of Lucius as senator
135	*standing*	a place to stand, an erection
135	*took an order with him*	for needlework, with implication that she brought him to climax so he no longer has a 'standing'
139	*stood bare*	in the open air, also naked
140	*pastery*	place where pastry/patisserie is made. There may be a joke on vaginal and anal sex in Gullman's tasting both the pastery and the pantry
146	*this giblet pie*	possibly a reference to Flavia's relationship with Lucius – the joining of giblets was synonymous with marriage
148	*hornpipe*	pipe with a mouthpiece made of horn – phallic ref.
148	*small mist*	proverbial for deception
151	*Man was asleep when woman's brain was made*	literally so in Genesis

2[.3]

9	*bribing sorcerors*	tricksters in whose interests it might be to disparage justice. MS reads 'philosophirs'
9	*blind*	usually suggests impartiality, but here also means unconcern, callousness
22	*gentleman-usher*	one who walks before a person of high rank, needs no skill
24	*glass*	mirror
27	*be lousy*	have lice
28	*antic*	foolish, lunatic
34	*put it up*	put up with it
39	*preferring*	support/advocacy of the petition
45	*monopoly*	exclusive rights to a trade, notoriously bestowed by James I on his favourites
45	*transportation*	licence to export
46	*concealment*	to hold land without a proper title to it

48	*corporation* company which controlled a particular trade
50	*Porters' Hall* London theatre built around 1615 but closed down by residents of the Blackfriars within three years. Important for dating the play
53	*roods* equivalent to one quarter of an acre
54	*sheep-walk* tract of land for grazing sheep
59	*mark* visible sign, perhaps specifically the tin badge worn by the porters' guild, also a blow
69 SD	*gallant* showy in appearance
71	*beaver* hat
75	*roses* rosettes on his shoes
75-6	*prick him forward* urge forward with something sharp i.e. the thorns of the roses
102	*Musaeus* mythical singer, famous for curing diseases and relating oracles
107	*Astraea* goddess of Justice, said to have fled the world in the Iron age
112	*idiot* ignorant, uneducated man
112	*garnish'd posts* decorated sign-posts
113	*sink* cesspool
117	*worm* silkworm, also hints at the worm which eats men's corpses
120	*piebald jays* black-and-white birds, proverbially associated with foolishness
120	*eagle's perch* high up, a symbol of majesty
134-5	*at a beck* with the slightest command or gesture
143	*Heart!* God's heart!
147	*an alms* donation of money to poor and needy
149	*groat* English silver coin worth fourpence
153	*faugh!* exclamation of scorn or disgust
155	*void* eject
158	*'Foot!* God's Foot!
169-70	*under-whores* subordinate, less expensive prostitutes
170	*upon the ticket* on credit

172	*try your back* under weight of prostitute
173	*eringo roots* root of the sea-holly thought to be an aphrodisiac, as were the following:
173-4	*doves's pizzles* doves's penises
174	*clary* herb, also good for the eyesight
174	*lambs's stones* lambs's testicles
175	*provoke* rouse to anger or sexual desire
177	*threescore* a man of sixty
179	*strange* unfamiliar, something associated with other people
180	*standing* reputation, with pun on erection
180	*be for thee* back to assist thee
183	*dastard* contemptible, cowardly
184	*on thy aged shoulders, bear* ref. to Atlas who supported the heavens on his shoulders. Vague echoes of *Hamlet*, 3.1.58-90
195	*superfluous humour* an excess of one of the four humours was thought to cause physical and mental disorders
195-6	*sound blood ... heart* perhaps healthier because lighter in colour
201	*sway* rule
202	*First Mover* God, who set the heavens in motion
204	*partless* impartial

3[.1]

0	SD The stage is divided into an upstage area where the Officers stand and Catzo and Gisbert first enter and a downstage where benches are set out to represent the Senate
0.1	SD *fitting* befitting, suiting
5	*are suitable to it* match his embroidered doublet
6	*my entrance much concerns me* it really matters to me to get in
17	*asper* a small, silver Turkish coin
19	*dotes* to be foolish (in old age), to love passionately

19	*of*	on
30	*rail*	complain bitterly
32	*physic*	medicine
33	*Insani*	Italian for 'insane'
83	*has only*	he has only
89	*seat*	his body
126	*deprave*	detraction, slander
127	*Bedlam*	St. Bethlehem's hospital for the insane in London
127	*tongue*	language associated with madmen; cf. Poor Tom, another Bedlamite, in *King Lear*
127	*please*	are pleased
129	*glass*	hourglass
132	*strange oppression*	external weight or pressure
142	*May I*	if I might
152	*put up*	put up with
154	*may be*	might be
156	*cedars*	trees famous for being tall and evergreen
160	*just aim'd*	corresponded exactly
162	*state*	statecraft or policy
167	*Have you now said?*	Have you said your piece?
172	*erst*	earlier
178	*Tush*	exclamation of disapproval or contempt
180	SD *He ascends the state*	this is unlikely to indicate use of the upper stage but rather Gisbert's taking his place where the Senate sat
189	*out of the way*	lost, in the wrong place
212	*empty-pated*	empty-headed
212	*painted idols*	blasphemous images of worship
213	*purpler*	colour of the senators' robes but also associated with blood i.e. the blood- or lust-stained consciences of the senators
218	*yon marble vault*	heaven. Hieronimo makes a similar appeal to the heavens in *The Spanish Tragedy*, 3.7.13-18
224	*jealousy*	not only envy but vigilance

224	*watch* stay awake during
224	*wanton* heedless, as well as sexually profligate
226	*ebon* ebony, black
227	*downy* feathery or fluffy, able to suffocate
228	*partial watch* watchmen who represent the senate's interests rather than those of Gisbert and Urania
230	*mock* counterfeit

3[.3]

6	*trow?* do you think?
7	*purgations* purifying rituals associated with magic
17	*commonwealth's man* good citizen, but also, in 1655 when the play was first published, an adherent of Cromwell's republic
20	*cousin-germanes* related as cousins
21-2	*Pick me a salad* proverbial for being engaged in some trivial task
24	*has as lief pick rushes* would as gladly pick rushes, proverbial for being worth nothing
28	*dismal* unlucky, sinister and dark, i.e. written in black
29	*characters* letters
30	*make away* murder
35-41	*night raven ... croaks* ravens were associated with revenge. Gisbert may here recall the line 'The croaking raven doth bellow for revenge' originally from the anonymous play, *The True Tragedy of Richard III* but more famously quoted in *Hamlet*, 3.2.241-2
35	*ha't* have it
35-6	*suit with* befit
37	*closets* small, private rooms
39	*draught* catch
42	*those made others* those who made others
45	*politician* one versed in the art of government or statesmanship

49	*charge*	instruction or admonition given to jury by a judge
51-2	*learning ... advanced*	scholarship was proverbially ill-rewarded. There may be an allusion here to Bacon's *The Advancement of Learning*, published in 1605
59	*He had a daughter*	Catzo might deliver this as a question but Gisbert responds as if the past tense had been stressed. Catzo may have heard that Urania is missing, presumed dead
63	*foolosopher*	term famous from Erasmus' *The Praise of Folly* for the fool who pretends to know philosophy
64	*Aristarchus*	could refer to either the Greek astronomer (3rd C BC) or the literary scholar and librarian at Alexandria (217-145 BC)
67-8	*made all of glass*	a common delusion of schizophrenics, manifested by Charles VI, King of France, whom Henry V defeated at Agincourt
72	*coxcomb*	fool
76	*to your books*	perhaps a reference to Aristarchus as librarian at Alexandria
77-8	*it will not save me*	although Protestantism advocated education for individual study of the Bible, Calvin's doctrine of predestination argued that this could not save man from his preordained fate
88-91	*corpus simplex ... element*	Gisbert describes the adulteration of the law through its function as a profit-making body
90	*composition*	combination, agreement of contract or treaty
95	*simple body*	physically ill-formed, plain
97	*she*	Justice
98	*broad cloth*	renowned for its cost as well as its width
99	*slender comings-in*	scant revenues or income
106	*ward*	a defensive posture or movement in fencing
107	*Have at you!*	opening attack in fencing
110	*rise upward*	advance socially and financially
113	*join issue*	join in controversy, i.e. start a fight

120	*light* sexually immoral, because easily persuaded or moved
121	*turns upward* turns onto her back
125	*carted* punishment for whores involved being whipped through the streets at the tail-end of a cart
126-7	*buys it out* pays off the authorities
128	*Lucullus* Roman consul, Epicurean and scholar in 1st C BC. Died insane
137	*participate* share in
139	*impartial* hostile
140	*obit* death
144	*Aesculapius* god of medicine and healing in Roman mythology
154	*king of the birds* eagle, a symbol of justice and majesty
158	*ope* open
158-9	*Will lay …loathe the light* Gisbert will either reveal all (unveiling night) or forever seek darkness himself
173	*'fence* defence
180	*schedule* written scroll or parchment, referring to the petition
181	*Recall thyself* come back to your senses
183	*man* i.e. not a god
189	*smart* pain
197	*forgetfulness* not just Gisbert's lack of courtesy to the King but his madness
198	*pinnacle* pyramid or spire
198	*made a god* referring to the pinnacle which reaches heaven and is immortal
202	*doom* judgement

4[.1]

5	*Out upon thee* expression of abhorrence or reproach
26	*harbinger* person who provides lodging i.e. the constable
27	*lodging at cost of the parish* in prison or poorhouse
44	*Oyez!* call by a public cryer

47	*mark* brand on a sheep to identify its owner. Also with a lewd pun on mark, signifying female genitals
51	*swimming* living in uncertainty, perhaps watery because suffused with tears
57	*ballad* popular song often attacking people or institutions
60	*bear parts* in singing the ballad, as well as hanging Lucius
61	*Contemn'd* despised
63	*obsequious right* fawning expression of duty
64-5	*motion is from the sun* the movement of a shadow is obviously dependent upon the sun; 'motion' is also used in its cosmological sense
65	*down once* i.e. when the sun has set
68	*Virtue poor* when Virtue has nothing to give in return
71	*leaden weight of time* pendulum of a clock
73	*observing* showing respect to greatness, conforming
74	*Greekish dame* Penelope, famed for her chastity whilst she waited for her husband, Ulysses, to return
76	*no foil* i.e. wealth, rank
76	*to put thy virtues off* set off thy virtues
77	*spin out thy days* Penelope spun a tapestry with which to delay her remarriage
78	*sell thy blood* 'blood' meaning flesh and, more specifically, hymeneal blood
81	*jealous* vigilant, possessive
82	*trust him with the night* Urania fears he will kill himself
84	*afford* yield
85	*suiting with* befitting
94	*sympathy* affinity in suffering
104	*seat* place where it resides in the body
105	*sway'd* since blood is continually circulating round the body, lust is fickle and wavering
109	*captiving* capturing
116	*how can you, sir?* (be well)
123	*alone* solely, also singly as Urania understands it

127	*pistolet*	gold coin, worth about 5 or 6 shillings
139	*ducats*	gold coins, worth about nine shillings

4[.2]

6	*Cavus*	seemingly the only reference to this figure in English Renaissance drama. MS spells it 'Corvus' which would suggest the 4th C BC Roman consul, M. Valerius Corvus, famous as an example of the favours of fortune, but not known as a shepherd
9	*covetous*	eager, desirous
14	*viands*	provisions
19	*'mends*	amends
27	*suck'd her dry*	image of Rage feeding from tigress until she has no milk left
36	*liquorish*	greedy
43	*better course*	i.e. Adelizia
44	*'scaped*	escaped
44	*mark*	target in archery
50	*broaching*	enlargement of a hole, i.e. deflowering
51	*for ripening*	as if, like fruit, she fell from the tree too early
56	*ye had a leak*	reason for shipwreck but also reference to menstruation, perhaps suggesting Adelizia is 'ripe'; that women were 'leaky' was a standard claim of early modern misogyny, often implying sexual incontinence
58-9	*let's down*	let's lie down/fall, sexually and morally
64	*Chaste Lucrece*	famous Roman matron, the archetype of chastity, who killed herself after she had been raped by Tarquin
69	*cuckold*	man whose wife has committed adultery
71	*prevent the fire*	punishment for adultery
72	*be stabbed*	pun on sexual intercourse
75	*should*	must
77-8	*enter into bonds ... articles*	legal process of marriage contract, here ironic because possibly preceding rape

94	*bellowing ox*	perhaps the Cretan bull which caused great destruction until Hercules captured it as his sixth task
137-8	*had nap*	surface given to fabric by raising fibres, as opposed to being threadbare, i.e. as long as the king was powerful and wealthy
140	*unmindful*	neglectful
171	*forfeiture*	penalty for transgression against the law
175	*demur upon't*	hesitate, express doubt about it
176	*We only want*	all we lack is
181	*gag'd*	offered as guarantee or forfeit

5[.1]

10	*impulsive*	assaulting, impelling
10	*attracting*	drawing in towards
13	*fain*	gladly
14-5	*good wine needs no bush*	proverbial, the practice of hanging ivy in tavern windows to advertise wine was for sale
21	*Thy worst*	Do thy worst!
25	*forbear him*	have patience with, spare him
27	*prefer'st the cart before the horse*	to set the cart before the horse was proverbial for something absurd, as well as out of sequence i.e. Urania becoming a bawd (*procuress*) before she has been a prostitute
30	*with a mischief*	an imprecation
36-7	*vaulting-school*	brothel
65	*surserare*	'with a siserara' was a common expression meaning with a vengeance, promptly. Also refers to the writ of *certiorari* by which one who had failed to get justice appealed to a higher court
75	*presently*	immediately
81	*flesh-fly*	blow-fly, feeds off dead flesh
82	*took no bribe*	because she gave it to him
96	*not unknown to*	in the carnal sense

5[.2]

2	*painted*	with cosmetics
5	*court me fair*	court me well or until I become fair
7	*for your turn*	to be made use of by you
7-8	*saucy jack*	rude knave
9	*engirt*	encircle
10	*stones*	jewels, testicles
14	*bolt*	Sigismond refers to the blow Alexis struck
19	*bravely*	splendidly
22	*pigsny*	term of endearment especially for a girl or woman
26	*sheep's eye*	a loving or timorous look
28	*thumb's length*	thumb used to penetrate sexually
29	*short allowance*	compared with a penis
34	*maw*	a card-game
34-6	*ace of hearts ... fingers on't*	bawdy joke perhaps with cards suggesting the shape of female and male genitalia
37	*noddy*	fool, simpleton
40	*tickled*	felt aroused
41	*conceit*	thought
43-4	*come over thee*	overcome, have sex with
46	*poting-stick*	used for crimping linen or stirring clothes when boiling, also here with phallic pun
48-9	*the true elements of a drunkard ... maudlin-like*	the stages of drunkenness defined as craftiness, belligerence and finally self-pity
53	*swell now*	arousal, especially male tumescence but also pregnancy
53	*lips*	also implies labial lips
54-5	*chop-cherry*	game in which player tries to catch a suspended cherry with his teeth
57	*parboil'd stuff*	half-boiled, since heat was supposed to force the genitals outwards in the male foetus, women were literally thought to be the product of insufficient heat
58	*hollow vessel*	this and the other containers (synonymous

	with female genitals) play on the idea of woman needing to be filled by man
58	*aqua-vitae* literally water of life, but associated with spirits
65	*Mars' standard* phallic ref.
66	*Venus' buckler* shield, but also vagina
70	*put up* put sword back in its sheath
72	*brain swims* through drunkenness
78	*pinnace* small, light boat
79	*fly-boat* small, fast-sailing boat
81	*Amain* lower the sail
85	*thrust out my bottom* reference to the threat of male rape in this scene
86-7	*a young courtier and an old beggar* proverbial, based on the courtier's famous extravagance
91	*All's one for that* it makes no difference
94	*on* of
94-5	*as many knights do* because they lack money or because they make this promise to prostitutes
96	*hotly …cool'd* temperatures suggest sexual arousal and then the waning of affection
96-7	*over head and ears* with ref. to sea water and perhaps sexual climax
100	*strange* foreign, unknown
104	*hart in rutting-time* deer in mating season
111	*fain deal withal* gladly entertain, also sexual reference
114	*lost you* made you mad
115	*they talk of countenances* the study of physiognomy was popular at the time

5[.3]

12	*the lists* place of combat
15	*forbids to* forbids me to
24	*depends* is waiting
40	*just mov'd* justly motivated

41	*principal* of most importance, also legal term meaning the chief person concerned in some proceeding or the perpetrator
51	*needs not* is not necessary
54	*three lives* the third seems to be Gisbert
57	*miserable* wretched, unworthy
64	*'void* avoid
65	*takes* catches hold
66	*utter* sell
69	*Christian burial* denied to prostitutes
71	*For those* prostitutes
71	*common* pun on common law and sexual availability
83-4	*how ... blood* i.e. they were so overwhelmed by happiness at finding one another, they can't possibly have been planning murder
86	*seeking her own ill* because she brought about her own death
99	*partless* impartial
101	*affection* personal inclination, partiality
104	*Strange and unheard of* in fact, this scene recalls Sidney's *Arcadia* where Euarchus condemns to death his own son and his nephew
113	*repriev'd* because it spared her punishment on earth
114	*feloniously* criminally
120	*dare not see* his eyes are blinded by tears
126	*fact* crime
135	*bear equal sail* remain impartial
153	*Hell's harbinger* Hell's host
155	*banish her* common punishment for prostitutes who would be banished from a particular parish
158	*continual progress* movement of Tudor and Stuart monarchs around the country, i.e. the bawd will be unhappy in the country unless her courtly clients come out to visit her
219	*challenge it* lay claim to it

Synopsis

The play takes place in Thessaly, seven years after the deposition of King Ferdinand. In the first scene, Lucius, an exiled courtier now disguised as a shepherd, is discovered wooing the shepherdess, Urania. Her father agrees to the match and settles all his belongings on the couple as a dowry. However, at the wedding celebrations, Lucius learns that King Ferdinand has defeated the usurper, Oswell, and has reclaimed his throne, subsequently recalling all those who suffered exile for his sake. Without explanation, Lucius abandons his new bride, sells Gisbert's lodge and flocks to a rival shepherd, and sets off for the court to reclaim his former identity. Homeless and destitute, Urania goes in search of Lucius, whilst Gisbert, the poor man of the play's title, goes in search of justice.

Meanwhile, Ferdinand's son, Sigismond, mad with grief at his father's deposition, has been left in the care of a servant, Catzo. In the forest they come across a young shipwreck-victim, the princess Adelizia. Sigismond falls instantly in lust and tries to assault her but is prevented by the arrival of Alexis, a shepherd who is searching for Urania. Adelizia and Alexis agree to remain in the forest together.

During this time, Urania (disguised as Castadora) has found a place in the house of a bawd, Mistress Gullman, and her daughter, Flavia. It is here that she encounters Lucius, now made a senator and courting Flavia unaware that she is a prostitute. Gisbert is also in the city pursuing justice. When he meets Lucius again, the latter denies all knowledge of him. Gisbert subsequently accuses his son-in-law of treachery before the whole senate but his pleas fall on deaf ears. Even if Gisbert had proof of Lucius' transgressions, the senators would not act: 'Poor men must suffer, rich do what they will'.

Gisbert, now mad with grief, meets Sigismond and Catzo and together they debate questions of justice. Ferdinand enters, lamenting the supposed death of Adelizia, the princess who was intended to marry his son. Gisbert explains the cause of his griefs to the King who immediately confronts Lucius and elicits a confession from him. Ferdinand then sentences Lucius to death unless he can recover Urania. He also banishes two of the guilty senators and appoints Gisbert as his Chief Justice.

Back in the forest, Adelizia comes across the defeated usurper, Oswell. His attempt to rape her is interrupted by the return of Alexis and the two banished senators. Oswell discovers Adelizia's identity and accuses her and Alexis of illicit sex, thus to provoke the wrath of her father, King Valerio, against Ferdinand in the hope of reinstating himself.

In the city, another outcast, Lucius, begs a lodging from the bawd and her daughter but is turned away. He is about to commit suicide when Urania discovers herself to him. She tells him that Flavia is really a prostitute and gives him money to spend the night with her that he may see for himself. The following morning there is an argument and Lucius kills Flavia.

In the final scene, Gisbert presides over the trial of Urania and Lucius. He condemns them to death but Ferdinand intervenes, pardoning both and banishing Mistress Gullman six miles from the city. Alexis and Adelizia enter; their case is to be judged by a combat between Alexis and the disguised Oswell. However, before the fight can begin, the two banished senators reveal Oswell's identity and his plot to discredit Adelizia. The King promises to reward Alexis and has Oswell taken away to prison. Meanwhile, Sigismond appears to have been restored to his wits and the play ends in anticipation of his marriage to Adelizia.

Textual Notes

This edition of *The Poor Man's Comfort* is based on the first published text of the play, the 1655 quarto (Q). Two copies of Q are to be found in the British Library: one published alone (shelfmark 644.d.61) and one bound with an edition of Daborne's other extant play, *A Christian Turned Turk* (shelfmark c.12.f.6). The former copy has been used for this edition.

The play also exists in manuscript form (MS) in a collection of fifteen plays in the British Library, MS. Egerton 1994, fols 268-92. It has been impossible to provide an accurate date for this manuscript. A reprint of MS has been published by the Malone Society, prepared by Kenneth Palmer (Oxford: Oxford University Press, 1955). Where Q is unclear or incomplete, I have referred to this reprint of MS.

The choice of Q as copy-text is based on the assumption that this edition was printed from the prompt book and that it therefore represents a closer approximation to the play as originally performed than MS which appears to have been based on scribal copy or copies of Daborne's foul papers. There are a number of reasons for assuming that Q is the more theatrical text, though which period of the play's performance history this represents cannot be judged with any certainty (see Editor's Introduction). The stage directions refer at one point to two actors, 'Sands' and 'Ellis' (1.2.4 SD), who seem to have taken the parts of the two Lords. Passages that appear in MS but not in Q look very much like theatrical cuts. They usually occur in long speeches and seem intended to remove material which fills out the background to the plot but adds little to the present action e.g. Oswell's description of his usurpation of Ferdinand (1.2.9-10, MS 204-18) or Urania's reminiscences of her courtship by Lucius (1.3.53, MS 430-41).

In general, MS bears signs of confusion where reworkings and crossings-out have not been made clear and the scribe has included both versions. However, passages where MS has been preferred over Q include Gisbert's speech in 2.3 (ll 102-25) where there appear to have been a number of substantive errors: 'sage' instead of 'didst', 'jawes' instead of 'jays' etc. MS has also been relied upon to clear up uncertainty over speech prefixes at 3.3.75 and 4.2.123 and to supply a line missing in Q at 3.1.104.

The following notes record all verbal emendations of the text and their sources with other significant departures in speech prefixes (SPs) and stage directions (SDs), but excluding minor changes in the positioning of the latter. Stage directions of editorial origin are enclosed in square brackets but without attribution, as most are both necessary and obvious. Readings originating in this edition are designated *this edn*. Q is divided into five acts but does not use scene divisions so these have been inserted, following the convention of beginning a new scene either when the stage has been cleared or when there is a change of location.

Spelling has been modernised in accordance with the principles outlined in the Editorial Board's Preface. There are a number of passages where it has been necessary to reline verse as prose and vice versa, sometimes with reference to the lineation of MS. Daborne often favoured end-rhymes at the expense of scansion and, tempting though it has been to improve the metre by relineation, this edition reflects this characteristic of Daborne's style.

1[.1]

17	has sung] *this edn;* has song Q, hath sung MS
40	and but hear] MS; but and hear Q
50	witness to] MS; witnesse Q
87	Wilt] *this edn;* Wo't Q, wut MS

Textual Notes

107	prayers] *this edn;* payers Q, prairers *MS*
109	I'll] *MS;* I Q
118	face] *MS;* fate Q
139	You] *MS;* Your Q
163	thee] *this edn;* the Q

1[.2]

4	SD *Enter two* LORDS] *this edn;* Enter 2 Lords, Sands, Ellis Q
24	SP *All*] *this edn;* Ors Q, orde *MS*
57	free] *MS;* fere Q
76	were] *MS;* are Q
88	hence] *this edn;* hens Q, henns *MS*

1[.3]

10	SD *Music*] *this edn;* Dance Q
11	Menalcas] *this edn;* Venalcas Q, Alexis *MS*
42	transports] *MS;* transport Q
88	One] *this edn;* I Q, a *MS*
118	wilt] *this edn;* wot Q, wut *MS*
130	will] *MS;* well Q

2[.1]

37	What not move yet?] *this edn;* What not - more yet? Q, not move yet *MS*
125	though] *MS;* thou Q
144	winds blow] *MS;* winde! blow Q

2[.2]

129	comes] *MS;* come Q

2[.3]

2	Justice's] *this edn;* Justice Q, *MS*
6	advocates] *this edn;* advocate Q, *MS*

9	Though] *MS;* The Q
16	others] *MS;* other Q
102	Musaeus] *this edn;* Nuseus Q, *MS*
103	experienced] *MS;* experience Q
103	didst] *MS;* sage Q
104	Foretell the] *MS;* Foretell till the Q
113	rottenness] *MS;* rottenlesse Q
120	Those] *MS;* his Q
120	jays] *MS;* jawes Q
124	Ha!] *MS;* Has Q
140	Ay] *this edn;* I Q, I know *MS*
156	thee] *this edn;* the Q, *MS*
162	you] *MS;* your Q
192	sights have] *this edn;* sighs have Q, sight hath *MS*

3[.1]

89	this man] *MS;* his name Q
101	her] *MS;* their Q
104	What … consent] *MS; this line missing in* Q
121	ingratefulness] *MS;* ingratitude Q. *MS restores rhyme*
168-9	Ha! …/ 'Tis … House] *this edn;* Ha! all gone, tis not possible./ Not possible? This … House Q; ha all gone not possible?/ this … howse *MS*
197	wilt] *MS;* wo't Q

3[.2]

0	SD *MS subst;* Q *adds* Enter Gisbert again

3[.3]

3	take it] *MS;* take Q
35	suit] *MS;* smite Q
64	Aristarchus] *MS;* Aristark asse Q
75	SP *Gisbert*] *MS; Sigismond* Q
111	an honest] *MS;* a honest Q

Textual Notes

135	SD *Enter ... OFFICERS*] *this edn; Enter Ferdinand, Vincentio, Glisco, Silleus* Q; *Enter* K: *Vincentio, Licugo,* MS
140	obit] *MS;* object Q
160	SD *Enter ... SILLEUS*] *this edn; Enter Lucius* Q; Enter lucius: silenis. leonard glisco *MS*

4[.1]

65	down] *this edn;* done Q

4[.2]

15	promises] *this edn;* promise Q, seemes to promise *MS*
49	under-vassal] *MS;* under vessell Q
69-70	in the morning] *MS;* the morning Q
88	will not] *MS;* wonot Q
123	SP *Alexis*] *MS;* Adelizia Q
144	did rise] *MS;* did did rise Q
150	gentlemen] *this edn;* Gentleman Q
155	only] *MS;* only but Q
159	Valerius'] *MS (valerios);* Valerius his Q
179	'em] *this edn;* 'um Q, them *MS*

5[.1]

28	turn'st] *MS;* turn Q
78	thy] *MS;* this Q

5[.2]

2	Ay] *this edn;* I Q, *MS*
43	will not] *this edn;* wo'not Q
65	Mars's] *this edn;* Mars his Q, *MS*
83	SD Enter FERDINAND ... GLISCO] *this edn;* Enter Ferdinand and others Q; Enter ferdinand vincentio licidaye *MS*

5[.3]

23	SD Exeunt … OSWELL …] *this edn; at 9 in* Q
47	immaculate] *MS;* Immaculates *Q*
68	whom's] *MS;* whom *Q*
78	whereof] *MS;* hereof *Q*
100	bestow'd] *MS;* bestows *Q*
141	SP *Ferdinand] MS; missing in Q*
162	SD] *at 166 in Q*
173	'Tis] *MS;* This *Q*
178	me] *MS; not in Q*
223	SP *Leonardo and Silleus] MS; Omnes Q*
235	end] *this edn;* ends *Q, MS*

The POOR-MANS COMFORT.

Act. I.

Enter Lucius like a Shepheard, and Urania like a Shepheardesse.

Luc. Stay fair *Urania*, thou whose only beautie
Would make a desert rich, and force Kings leave
Their purple thrones, to come and gaze at thee.
Lisander craves thee stay, he that does dote on thee,
More then the female on her new faln kid.

Ura. You should be still a flatterer by your tongue.

Luc. By all my hopes I swear, returne my love
But that fair grace it merits, and on my faith
A tryal, beyond which the covetous thought
Of man nere went, Ile undergoe;
And in the Achievement lose my self ere thee.

Ura. You overvalue me, were I possest
Of so high passions, what you terme love;
Alexis equal suit should sooner move
Then you, whose birth is all unknown to me.

Luc. Ungentle maid, let not thy cruelty
Force me despair, he that so oft has song
And won the prize for dance and roundelayes;
He that has vowed his chast thoughts to thy shrine,
Given thee the tender firstlings of his flocks;
Who amongst the fairest Lasses of the plains,
Chose thee his prize, when at the publick games,
He crown'd thee with the wreath, which for his merit
In songs and active sports he did inherit,
From the deserving swaines; Do not forget
My seven years service, which to attain thee yet,
Would seem but as one Summers day.

Ura. You are too forward.

Luc. True love does charge, and that fault lay on me;
Oh did thy yeelding heart feel but the fires!

Ura. Alas! I feel too much, in modesty forbear
Thy violent suit, which breeds suspect; true love being ever mute,
When lust findes means to speak.

B *Luc.*

Facsimile of *The Poor Man's Comfort* (London, 1655), fol. B1.
Reproduced by permission of the British Library (644.d.61)